SOUTH CAROLINA WOMEN

ALSO BY IDELLA BODIE:

SOUTH CAROLINA
WOMEN
IDELLA BODIE

SANDLAPPER PUBLISHING, INC.

ORANGEBURG, SOUTH CAROLINA

Revised Edition 1991
First Paperback Edition 1991
Second Printing 1994

Printed in the United States of America

Published by Sandlapper Publishing Co., Inc., Orangeburg, South Carolina 29115

Book design by Linda Benefield

Library of Congress Cataloging in Publication Data

Bodie, Idella.
    South Carolina women / by Idella Bodie. — 1st ed.
        p. cm.
    Includes bibliographical references and index.
    ISBN 0-87844-079-8. — ISBN 0-87844-102-6 (pbk.)
    1. Women—South Carolina—Biography. 2. South Carolina—History.
3. Leadership. I. Title.
CT3260.B62 1991
920.72'09757—dc20
                                                                    90-48424
                                                                        CIP

For Jim

Foreword

Over ten years have passed since the first edition of *South Carolina Women* was published, time for an entire generation of young people to pass through the educational system of our state. The first edition filled a long-felt need for information on famous women in South Carolina which would be suitable for students in the schools.

This edition has been expanded with additional information on earlier women, as well as the inclusion of others. The author, Idella Bodie, is to be congratulated for her extensive research, which brings vitality to these vignettes. In every way this edition lives up to its predecessor.

It is our hope that young people who read these lives will be better informed on the important role women in South Carolina played in the history of our state and be inspired to emulate some of their achievements.

MARGARET W. EHRHARDT

Former Library Consultant
S.C. Department of Education
Columbia, South Carolina

Preface

In the spring of 1977, Mrs. Margaret Ehrhardt, at that time Library Consultant for the public schools of South Carolina, visited Aiken High School where I was a teacher of English. Knowing of my writing for young people, she requested that I consider helping to supply the needs of South Carolina youth by compiling information about the women of our state.

After much consideration and a blessing from my publisher, I undertook the task. As a result, *South Carolina Women: They Dared to Lead* came out in the fall of 1978.

South Carolina Women is a revised edition of this earlier publication. New information has been included in the earlier vignettes, and twenty new sketches have been added, making a total of more than fifty women.

To be sure, no one volume could possibly do justice to all the deserving "Palmetto" women. They not only make individual contributions, but many multi-talented women form countless associations and clubs that donate their time to improve our state and its citizens. Still other women, like Martha Laurens Ramsey, serve as exemplars of motherhood. They all deserve our praise. To in part atone for not being able to include all worthy persons, I have listed more than one hundred and fifty women of achievement in the latter portion of the book. Another volume could perhaps highlight these women and others.

As with the first edition, I have researched in libraries over South Carolina and consulted librarians, teachers, and historians in an effort to present a fair representation of the women who have contributed to our state, and for that matter, to our nation.

In order to assist the young reader in placing each individual in her background, I have divided the book into chronological historical periods. I have also attempted to present the women in a manner that young readers might identify with in their struggle to achieve in a world often geared toward males.

My hope is that *South Carolina Women* will give a greater knowledge and understanding of the part women have played in the history of our great state. I further hope this work will encourage additional research from the bibliographical listings. More importantly, my desire is that this volume will instill pride in young females and thus inspire them to set high goals and work toward achieving those goals.

One of the most pleasant aspects of writing *South Carolina Women* has been the people I've been privileged to work with. I am grateful to all of these persons for their cooperation and encouragement. Of course I express gratitude to Mrs. Margaret Ehrhardt, who sparked the original flame. My appreciation also to Frank Handal, my publisher, for his faith in me as a writer; Miss Mary Frances Griffin, formerly with the State Department of Education; Dr. Lewis P. Jones of Wofford College; Dr. George C. Rogers, Jr., of the University of South Carolina; Professor Louise Pettus of Winthrop College; Dr. Tom Johnson, Herb Hartsook, Charles Gay, and other staff members of the South Caroliniana Library; Nancy Vance Ashmore and Walter Edgar of Southern Studies; the staffs of the following libraries: South Aiken High, Aiken County, Cooper, Fireproof Building, USC Aiken, and Charleston County; Representative Irene Rudnick; Sandra McKinney, Clerk of the House of Representatives; Elizabeth Verner Hamilton; Rose Wilkins; Editors Delmar Roberts, Linda Benefield, and Nancy Drake; Anne Sawyer, a faithful research companion, and members of the First Thursday Writers' Club.

Contents

COLONIAL TIMES

In 1682 several women looked from the low bluff of Albemarle Point (afterward called Charles Town; later, Charleston) upon the wilderness around them. These women were among the 160 persons who under a grant from King Charles II of England had come to settle in the Colonies, or the New World.

Just beyond the wilderness with a river on one side and a creek on the other lurked wild animals and men with "shaven heads and painted faces." What did these mothers of Carolina feel as they looked around? Did they envision comfort and happy homes for their children, or did the anticipated trials ahead fill their hearts with anxiety? However they may have felt, they spoke no word of fear. Their letters tell of their hardships but never of despair.

In later years these women and others of colonial times are often portrayed as shy, sweet, and prettily dressed, as well as being protected from physical labor by their husbands. Fiction has them sitting quite helplessly on verandas, where they sip lemonade and faint under stress. On the contrary, colonial women were hard workers. They kept gardens; tended farm animals; milked cows; made lard, soap, and candles; and did their own weaving and sewing. And, if the occasion arose, they managed plantations with hundreds of slaves. Some widows successfully continued their husbands' businesses.

The following women, whose acts of bravery and leadership have been recorded, represent the South Carolinians who helped to form our nation.

Judith Giton Manigault

MOTHER OF A NATION
1665–1711

The sound of Judith's ax echoed in the forest. Nearby her husband, Noe Royer, wielded a whipsaw.

Having escaped her native land for America, French Huguenot Judith Giton toiled beside her weaver husband. Together they felled trees and grubbed soil.

Judith's life is typical of the hardships endured in 1685 by some of South Carolina's first women. Judith wrote in a letter mailed abroad, "I have been six months without tasting bread, working like a ground slave; and I have even passed three and four years without having food when I wanted it."

When Judith's first husband died, she married Pierre Manigault, who operated a distillery and cooperage. Judith kept boarders, and she and Pierre laid the basis for prosperity.

When their son was seven, Judith died without knowing she was leaving the foundation for a great family. For Pierre and Judith's merchant son Gabriel built one of the fortunes in colonial America. His own son Peter became a member of the Commons House.

Affra Harleston Coming

LANDHOLDER
CIRCA 1649–1698

Affra's heart pounded under the cape drawn to protect her from the dampness of the sea air. She clutched her baggage and addressed the captain of the *Carolina*, which was anchored close by the *Port Royal* and the *Albemarle*.

"I want to go to Carolina with you, Sir," she said.

Judging from Affra's appearance, the captain determined she was "lady born."

"Why, Miss," he said, "the trip is not for the likes of you."

If he only knew, thought Affra, *that I have only four shillings in my pocket*. Since her father had lost everything by siding with the King of England against Cromwell, she and her brother felt compelled to go on the Port Royal expedition to mend their family fortune.

At her insistence in going, the captain asked his mate, John Coming, to arrange a male sponsor for her. "He will receive money for bringing you over," John said, "and after two years of employment with this sponsor you will be given one hundred acres."

With her family in Ireland left penniless, Affra had no choice. The crudeness of the women's quarters on board ship and the strange talk of some of the men did not deter her. She found that carrying her Bible helped with the latter problem. Too, she worried that her brother Charles was not aboard the *Carolina*.

Mate Coming helped to ease her fears by telling her Charles was probably a passenger on another of the ships, and often the two met at the bow to talk. Other passengers with whom she felt a kindred spirit were Joseph West, who was to become governor, and Stephen Bull and his brother.

After a long journey, a storm drove the *Carolina* into the island of Nevis, where Henry Woodward, a ship's surgeon and one of the earliest English settlers, joined them for a return trip to Carolina. There Affra learned that her brother Charles had sailed on another ship.

When Affra's servitude was completed in 1672, she and John Coming were married. The couple had a home, Comingtee, on the Cooper River. John became captain of the *Blessing* and continued to work for many years. While he was away, Affra managed the plantation.

John, now a member of the Grand Council and owner of much property, gave land for Oyster Point. After John's death Affra built a home in Charleston on the corner of Wentworth and Saint Philip Street. By her own resolution Affra willed seventeen acres of land to Saint Philip's Church. This transaction marked the beginning of parsonage property in South Carolina. Other property went to John H. and Isaac Bull.

Affra died December 28, 1698, and is buried at Comingtee beside John.

Henrietta Deering Johnston

PASTELIST
CIRCA 1670–1729

"My dear Henrietta," said her clergyman husband, "I cannot for the life of me see how you can dally so much at this frivolous pastime."

Henrietta stood back to study the delicate shading along the cheekbone of her subject. "Perhaps one day," she said, "my art will develop into something worthwhile."

"I cannot see how that is possible. In fact, I see no earthly resemblance whatsoever of the subject on the paper to anyone I know."

Despite her husband's constant criticism of her works, Henrietta Johnston continued to paint. The earliest American pastelist, Henrietta had come to South Carolina from Ireland in 1707 as the wife of an Irish clergyman, Gideon Johnston. As was natural in her time, her social and economic position depended chiefly on her husband. He became rector of Saint Philip's and Bishop of

London's Commissary in South Carolina.

Upon his death in a drowning accident in 1716, Henrietta supported her family by painting portraits of local dignitaries, as well as rich planters, officials, military men, and belles and beaux of the day in all their splendor of dress. Since she had no studio, she went to the subjects' homes to do much of her work.

Her portrait of Colonel William Rhett, painted in 1711, is in the Gibbes Art Gallery in Charleston; four others are in the Museum of Early Southern Decorative Arts in Winston-Salem, North Carolina. Two oval pastel portraits, valued at $30,000 since they are national treasures, hang in the South Carolina Governor's Mansion. One is the second wife of Robert Brewton; the other, the first wife of Charles Pinckney. Around fifty of her works are believed to exist in collections and museums in England and America.

America's first woman artist and pastelist is buried near her Beaufain Street home in the churchyard of Saint Philip's in Charleston.

Elizabeth Ann Timothy

JOURNALIST
CIRCA 1700–1757

Elizabeth wiped her perspiring brow with an ink-smudged hand. Then she held the little grayish sheet with its black lettering up before her and read

South Caroliniana Library

aloud: "Subscriptions will be kindly pleased to continue their favours to the poor afflicted widow with six small children and another hourly expected."

The year was 1738, and Elizabeth Timothy had just published a newspaper, the first by a woman in American journalism. Elizabeth's husband, French Huguenot Louis Timothy (Anglicized from Timothée), suffered a fatal accident after five years of printing the *South Carolina Gazette*. The public responded to Mistress Timothy's appeal.

In the fall of 1733, the family—including four children ages one through six—had sailed south to Charleston so that Timothy could take over one of Benjamin Franklin's newspapers after the editor died of yellow fever. Here Timothy received a land grant of 600 acres.

In spite of Louis's untimely death, Franklin could not have been more pleased with Elizabeth's handling of the newspaper. Of her he said: "She not only sent me as clear a state as she could find of the transactions past, but continued to account with greatest regularity and exactness to every quarter afterwards. She managed the business with such success that she not only brought up respectably a family of children but was able to purchase of me the printing house and establish her son in it."

It was said that Elizabeth Timothy had been "born and bred" in Holland, where knowledge of accounts was part of female education.

When her son Peter became of age, Elizabeth turned over the responsibilities of editor and printer to him and opened a shop next door. A 1746 advertisement read: "Pocket Bibles, Primers, Hornbooks, *Reflections on Courtship and Marriage, Pamela*." Poor Richard's almanacs were popular in the store.

After Peter's death, his wife Ann followed in her mother-in-law's footsteps. She, too, became printer of the *Gazette* and operated the shop with the addition of all writing material, fans, necklaces, handkerchiefs, gloves, and other accessories.

In 1800 the paper was replaced by the *Charleston Courier*.

Hannah English Williams

BIOLOGIST
1692–1722

"I have sent you some of our vipers and several sorts of snakes, scorpions and lizards in a bottle and I would have sent you a very good collection of plants if I had any vollums of brown paper.

"I have sent you a box with different shells and a nest made by a wild bee.

"Next spring I will send you some mocking birds and red birds. If I should send you any now the cold would kill them."

Hannah Williams

On the basis of this letter to James Petiver, head of the British Museum, Hannah English Williams is recorded as South Carolina's first woman biologist.

Sophia Wigington Hume

RELIGIOUS LEADER
1702–1774

"Sophia, I absolutely forbid you to go out wearing that horrifying red shawl!" Her mother's keen voice pierced the air. "What will people think of you and of me for allowing it?"

"I'm sorry, Mother." Sophia twirled around, flaring the fringe of her shawl, and ran her slender fingers in a scale along the piano keys. "I must follow my own instincts. I'm off to an afternoon of music, and my clothing must match my high spirits."

Susanna Wigington was the daughter of Mary Fisher, a famous Quaker minister, and her daughter's wearing of bright apparel and jewelry, taking music lessons, and attending fashionable amusements caused her much concern. Such behavior was prohibited by the Quaker Society.

Sophia's father, Henry, was an Episcopalian. And Sophia, by her own admission, was brought up in the ways of the world.

In 1721 Sophia married Robert Hume, a well-to-do Charlestonian, and continued to live a life of luxury and gaiety. The couple had two children, Susanna and Alexander.

During an illness Sophia began to change her way of thinking. Frivolities, she began to believe, endangered her soul. Only if she gave up her manner of living—forsaking her vanity and burning or selling her finery—would God spare her. Sophia's family and friends were upset about her decision.

A second crisis came with the death of her husband. At this time Sophia moved to England. There she joined the Society of Friends.

In 1747 she felt a divine call to return to Charleston, where she humiliated herself on the scene of her former elegance by calling for repentance. Friends in Philadelphia helped her raise money to publish a book, *An Exhortation to the Inhabitants of the Province of South Carolina*, which preached against luxury and appealed for repentance and reformation.

Thus, Sophia began her twenty-five-year travels over the Colonies distributing tracts, writing, and preaching. She began to receive increasing respect for her ministry and the strength of her intense prose.

In 1763 she published *A Caution to Such as Observe Days and Times*, written to denounce religious festivals.

In spite of her career as a minister and a writer, Sophia preached that a woman should devote herself to her home and church.

As the fellowship of Friends began to dwindle, Sophia embarked for England, where her daughter now lived. Though compelled to rest her slight and ailing body, she managed to preach to large public meetings.

Sophia Wigington Hume died January 26, 1774, in London. She was interred in Friends' Burial Ground near Bunhill Fields.

Martha Daniel Logan

HORTICULTURIST
1702–1779

In 1753 the *South Carolina Gazette* carried Martha Logan's advertisement: "A parcel of very good seed, flower roots, and fruit stones to be sold on the Green near Trott's Point."

Martha's early education, like that of most young women of her day, included reading, writing, and needlework. But Martha also enjoyed working with flowers and plants, for her father was in the nursery business. Robert Daniel, one of the last of the proprietary governors, died when his daughter was thirteen years old. Perhaps Martha inherited his business, as she did land along the Wando River.

Shortly after her father's death, Martha married George Logan, Jr. The couple had eight children. During this period Martha advertised in the *Gazette* that she would board students and tutor them at their Wando River home. Somewhat later she worked in a boarding school in Charleston.

Still, Martha's chief interest lay in gardening. She had known a Mrs. Lamboll, one of the first to have a garden in Charleston, and may have studied with her. At any rate, gardening rapidly became a fashionable hobby of the time, and wealthy ladies and gentlemen were very much interested in planting their grounds with rare plants and shrubs. As a result of her interest, Martha printed a "Gardener's Kalendar," and wrote a treatise on gardening that was published in 1752 in John Tobler's *South Carolina Almanack*.

In her nursery business, Martha took advantage of the ships that sailed from Charleston to Philadelphia. The good-natured captains would carry large tubs planted with roots and cuttings of all kinds.

John Bartram, a noted biologist with whom Martha exchanged seeds, wrote to a London correspondent: "Mrs. Logan's garden is her delight." Along with their correspondence a "little silk bagg," crammed with seeds, went back and forth between Charleston, Philadelphia, and London.

Once Martha wrote Bartram: "I have lost my bulbs for tulips and hyacinths. I had them in a closet to dry and the mice ate them."

South Carolinians also enjoyed Martha's nursery business. One woman wrote in her diary in 1763 of having been to Mrs. Logan's to buy roots.

Whether or not her nursery was profitable, Martha Logan's life was a rewarding one. She had family, friends, and flowers. It was because of her flowers that she has gained a place in the history of American gardening.

Mrs. Logan died in Charleston on June 28, 1779, and was buried in the family vault, since destroyed, in Saint Philip's churchyard.

Eliza Lucas Pinckney

INDIGO PLANTER
1722–1793

Sixteen-year-old Eliza Lucas looked at the parchment in her father's hand. Panic filled her heart.

"Papa," she addressed Major Lucas, "what is it?"

Love and sadness swept over his face. "Sit down, Eliza. We have much to discuss."

Eliza had never seen her father look so serious. Having inherited estates from his father in South Carolina, Major Lucas had just begun to instruct the slaves in the developing of his land on Wappoo Creek near the Ashley River.

The Lucas family had been happy in their new home. The climate was more favorable for frail Mrs. Lucas than that of Antigua in the West Indies. Eliza loved the giant oaks with their Spanish moss, the violets, and the fragrant yellow jessamine tangling over the fertile land. She especially liked the mockingbirds. Would they have to leave all this?

Eliza's blue lutestring gown spread around her as she sat on the settee in the spacious drawing room. She waited for her father to speak.

"Eliza, it really is not fair for me to ask this of you at your age, but I have no other choice." Lines of worry furrowed his brow. "By the orders of the King of England, I must return to my regiment in the West Indies. I want you to assume the responsibility of our three plantations, your mother, and your sister."

Eliza took a quick breath before she said, "I will do my best, Papa." Then she threw her arms around his neck and struggled to choke back the tears. There had always been a closeness between Major Lucas and this delicate-featured girl with red-gold hair. Of the four children, two sons had been left in England at a boarding school, and Polly was much too young to concern herself with the care of the plantation.

"Most of all, Eliza," he continued, "I want you to be patient with your mother. You know she is not well."

"How is Mamma taking the news?"

"She is upset. I must leave in the morning. If you need advice before a letter can reach me, go to our good friend Charles Pinckney or to Mr. Deveaux."

For a while they were silent. Then her father said, "Eliza, I want you to have contact with young people. I should like you to meet Captain Rippon. He is of a nice English family."

"Now, Papa—" Eliza's blue eyes twinkled. "Don't try to marry me off. After I learn more about what crops are best suited for our land, there will be time for social affairs."

Major Lucas responded with a deep glow of pleasure.

Eliza assumed the duties left by her father with a maturity far beyond her years. One of her first tasks was to build a nursery for the slave children and an infirmary for their ill. She saw, too, that their slaves had a balanced diet. For tending their needs, the slaves gave Eliza their love and respect.

Although Mrs. Lucas disapproved of her daughter's doing a man's work, Eliza was up and out every day at the first streak of dawn. Her day began with the inspection of the three plantations—Wappoo, Waccamaw, and Garden Hill. Then she discussed her findings with the overseers. Afterward, she devoted several hours to her music and books. She also taught her sister and some of the slave children. In the afternoons she went over reports from the overseers and sent these reports to her father. Each day had its schedule, and Eliza never allowed herself to be idle.

Nearly a month after Major Lucas sailed for Antigua, Eliza received a package of seed from him. His accompanying letter read: "Indigo has done well in Jamaica, and I am anxious for you to try it in South Carolina."

At the time rice was the chief crop, and Major Lucas felt it would mean much to the Province of South Carolina to be able to export indigo.

Eliza was excited about the prospect of growing indigo, although some of

Workers threshing rice, the major crop of the Pinckneys

the neighboring farmers tried to discourage her.

"Late frost and caterpillars," Mr. Deveaux pointed out, "are the enemies of indigo. Besides, the task of gathering the plants and extracting the dye is a tedious one."

None of the warnings influenced Eliza. She had high hopes of proving that a fine quality of indigo dye could be produced in the new settlement of South Carolina.

In the spring, with much painstaking care, she selected a few acres near the Wappoo house and supervised the planting of the round, yellow seed. She found it exciting to watch the seed dropped in the sandy loam trenches made by a hoe. For two days from dawn to dark she stayed in the field.

Mrs. Lucas openly opposed her daughter's actions. "Why not let the overseers do that?" she cried. "You should be accepting invitations that are coming in from eligible young men in Charleston."

A neighbor also criticized Eliza for getting up at five o'clock. "It will make you look old," she told Eliza, "and then you'll never get a husband."

Eliza's concern, however, remained with the indigo and the plantations. Her work was arousing much interest in surrounding areas, and many of the other planters came to watch her indigo experiments. One particularly interested gentleman was her father's friend Colonel Charles Pinckney, who shared Eliza's love for the outdoors.

Colonel Pinckney and his wife had no children; thus, they became extremely fond of Eliza. The colonel brought Eliza his books to read, including books of law.

Eliza's sparkling personality drew many admirers. One young man in particular often visited Wappoo—the Captain Rippon whom her father had spoken of. He shared Eliza's love of music, and he, Eliza, and Polly sang together. Mrs. Lucas, who was feeling much better now, enjoyed the young people and talked of marriage to Eliza.

Eliza, however, was not interested in marriage. She felt her life was far too complicated already. Along with indigo, she now planted ginger and fig trees. At her request for more schooling—the only formal education she had received was four years in England—an instructor from Charleston came out three days a week to hold classes for her and Polly.

Indoors, too, Eliza spent time writing letters: reports to her father and letters to her younger brothers still in school in England, as well as to her former teacher and friends in the Province. Eliza kept copies of all the letters she wrote, and they have been published in *The Letterbook of Eliza Lucas Pinckney.*

In late August Eliza's indigo was ready for cutting. Above the deep green leaves, purple-red stalks shot up about three feet. Slaves cut the plants just before blooming time and tied them in small bundles. Inside sheds, they plunged the bundled plants into large vats of warm water. After the indigo turned yellow, they transferred the plants to still another vat where they stirred them back and forth with long bamboo poles. At the appointed time the indigo was allowed to settle. Afterward, it was boiled, drained, and pressed into molds to dry.

Colonel Pinckney and Mrs. Deveaux came to watch the tedious operation.

Unfortunately, Eliza's first attempt at making the blue dye failed. She wrote to her father: "Perhaps the plants were harvested too soon or the temperature in the vats was not just right. At any rate, I want to try again, and next time I should like to plant the seeds sooner."

As Christmas holidays approached, Eliza received many invitations to dinners and balls in town houses in Charleston and mansions along the Cooper and Ashley rivers. Although Eliza danced the minuet until the musicians stopped playing, she did not shirk her responsibilities on the plantations. She supervised the crops, saw to the needs of the slaves, and wrote her father regularly.

With the coming of spring, Eliza became excited over her second planting of indigo. By June she was sure this year's crop would be successful. Field hands rose at sunrise to inspect each green leaf for caterpillars.

On the late August night before the indigo was to be harvested, everything was in readiness. Fires glowed beneath each great vat where a servant was stationed to check temperatures. Eliza did not close her eyes all night long. Work began at dawn and continued under lanterns and torches throughout the night.

When the juice had been extracted from the stalks and hardened into cakes, it was a "true blue." Eliza was jubilant. It was 1741. Eliza was nineteen, and the blue dye she had made from indigo had never before been successfully produced in South Carolina.

At this time Charles Pinckney's wife died following a lengthy illness. Eliza had always held great respect and admiration for this lawyer friend of the family, who was seventeen years older than she. In 1744 he and Eliza were married. Throughout their married life on his nearby plantation, Belmont, Eliza continued to call him Mr. Pinckney.

Eliza's father expressed his pleasure over the marriage and requested that Colonel Pinckney assume the responsibility of his plantations. Indigo soon became a profitable crop, and Eliza began experimenting with silkworms. Together the couple planted trees—mulberries, magnolias, and any foreign species they could obtain.

For a wedding gift Colonel Pinckney built his wife a plum-colored brick home in Charleston, which Eliza planned. They named the home Colleton Square. Dinners with venison and turkey became special occasions in Charleston, for Eliza was a perfect hostess. The house was lavished with flowers and fruit that Eliza grew.

Mrs. Lucas and Polly had joined Major Lucas in Antigua now, and they regularly shipped tropical plants to the Pinckneys.

Three children—two boys and a girl—soon blessed the Pinckney household. When, in 1753, Colonel Pinckney was appointed a colonial agent by Governor James Glen, the family went abroad so the boys could be educated in England.

Here Eliza's charm and wit brought popularity.

From South Carolina she brought a parakeet and a beautiful dress made from silk grown and woven at Belmont. She presented these to the Dowager Princess of Wales.

After five years abroad, the Pinckneys returned home on an exhausting ten-week voyage. They found their fields overgrown and the plantations in need of repair. Canals from the Cooper River, which controlled water to the rice fields, were choked with weeds. Due to overwork and contracting of malaria, Colonel Pinckney died.

Eliza returned to her passion for "gardening," as she called it, assuming full responsibility for the plantations. The Negroes respected her fairness; therefore, she was able to get an overseer and the cooperation required to restore the plantations.

At this time Charleston was alive with balls, concerts, and dinners, and Eliza once more became a part of this life. On Friday afternoons she held open house for the leaders of the Province. Their discussions included politics, crops, imports, and news from London. Unusual for a woman of that day, Eliza entered in the discussions. Although her formal education had been scanty, she had read widely and had extensive experiences. Coupled with her inquisitive nature, this background made her an interesting conversationalist. She was, however, worried about the talk of separating from England. Her sons, who had been brought up as Englishmen, were now grown, and Eliza felt close to England, to their many friends and relatives there.

When the war did erupt between England and the Colonists, Eliza's sons— Charles Cotesworth and Thomas Pinckney—became officers in the Revolutionary Army. During this time Eliza took refuge at Hampton Plantation on the South Santee, the home of her daughter, Harriet. (Archibald Rutledge, poet laureate of South Carolina, is one of her many descendants. He later lived at Hampton Plantation. In 1971 the home was sold to South Carolina. It is now a state park.)

In spite of her age, Eliza continued to be lively, enjoying her grandchildren and even entertaining George Washington.

In 1793 an illness sent her to consult a doctor in Philadelphia. She died there and was buried in Saint Peter's churchyard. By his own request George Washington was a pallbearer.

Unlike Eliza's vegetable dye from indigo, the dyes of today are developed from chemicals. Still, the state of South Carolina owes a debt of gratitude to Eliza Lucas Pinckney. Indigo was of great economic importance to the economy of South Carolina prior to the Revolution and during the founding of the nation. Through her repeated efforts to grow indigo and other plants unusual to our state, Eliza helped to found a new nation.

REVOLUTIONARY WAR TIMES

Since more battles of the Revolutionary War occurred in South Carolina than in any other state, the women found themselves in the midst of the conflict. Even during a lull between battles, the division among the citizens caused problems. Many Patriots, or "Whigs" as they were called, had to contend with the Loyalists, or "Tories," in their communities. Also, skirmishes between the Colonists and those who remained loyal to the mother country often pitted neighbor against neighbor.

Because the British had no posts in this country, they took over private homes—most often stately mansions—to set up their headquarters. Forcing family members into smaller living areas, the British officers squandered the Colonists' wealth. Homes not used in this way suffered the ravages of war. Soldiers ripped open feather mattresses to use the ticking for tent cloths and tore apart furnishings in search of hidden valuables.

Many of the women whose husbands were away fighting or those already widowed remained with their homes in hopes of saving some of their possessions. Consequently, they suffered abuse from the Tory soldiers.

Under these hardships the women of South Carolina showed courage and loyal commitment to their men and the noble cause for which they fought. Some carried messages in the face of danger; others protected family members at the risk of their own lives.

During a time in which women were expected to stay in the background, one woman—through unselfish service—made a lasting contribution to the world of art.

Rebecca Brewton Motte

PATRIOT
1738–1815

Rebecca Brewton Motte and her niece struggled under a clumsy pile of their personal belongings. In spite of her burden, Mrs. Motte pulled her petite body to its fullest height. She would not lose her dignity.

The British could force her to move from her lovely home and into the rough, weather-boarded overseer's house, but they would not daunt her pride.

She had not minded the Colonies' own Lieutenant Colonel Henry Lee's using her new mansion overlooking the Congaree River as his headquarters. She even invited him to do so and had shown his men every manner of hospitality, but this . . .

"Here, let me help you."

It was Captain McPherson, the British officer who was using her home as a garrison for his soldiers.

Turning, Mrs. Motte noticed her niece was carrying a handsome bow and arrows, a gift of a sea captain from the West Indies. An arrow had slipped from the quiver. McPherson had picked it up and was about to feel the point of it.

"Stop, Captain!" Mrs. Motte heard her niece say. "The arrows are poisoned, and it might cost your arm or your life if one should prick you."

"If only he were not so mannerly," thought Mrs. Motte, "I could be angrier with him."

Besides forcing her to move, he had his troops dig a ditch around her lovely home, making a high embankment to defend themselves. Worse still, they named it British Fort Motte.

It was a blessing her husband, Jacob Motte, had not lived to see this. She smoothed wisps of curling hair escaping the tightly drawn bun underneath the high-crowned mobcap. Her white square neckerchief, pinned down in front, was just as fresh as always, and black silk mittens covered her arms where the fitted sleeves ended.

At least she still had her faithful slaves, and she would manage the inconvenience. With this attitude she went about her duties as best she could, her full skirts swishing. From her waist dangled a silver chain from which hung her pin cushion, scissors, and a bright bunch of keys.

In the meantime Lee and Francis Marion had learned of McPherson's garrison and had become determined to attack him before Lord Rawdon could come to his aid. Realizing their small cannon could not dislodge him, they knew the only chance to make him surrender was to burn the house.

Lee, however, had not forgotten Mrs. Motte's kindnesses to him and his men. How could he ask her to let him burn her home!

Before Lee could announce his intention, Rebecca Motte herself brought him the bow and arrows that had been a gift.

"Colonel Lee," she said, "do not hesitate a moment. Not only do I give you my permission to burn my house, but I give you something to facilitate the destruction."

Standing before the speechless colonel, Mrs. Motte continued: "Tie burning tow to these arrows and shoot them onto the roof."

Several days later a strong-armed soldier manned the arrows. As Mrs. Motte had suggested, he tied hemp soaked in turpentine to the point, lighted it, and shot the flaming darts.

Richard Taylor

The weather was hot and dry. In moments smoke rose from the shingles. The housetop crackled and blazed.

Upon McPherson's orders British soldiers climbed onto the roof and began ripping off the blazing shingles. They could not afford to let the fire reach the powder stored inside. Shortly, American gunfire and the heat from the flames forced them to surrender. A white flag shot up to replace the British colors. After surrender, soldiers of both sides rushed to help extinguish the flames, and only the roof was burned.

Always kind and motherly, Mrs. Motte invited both American and British officers to eat the food she had prepared.

At dinner Captain McPherson said, "I was warned of the poisoned arrow; it would have been a blessing to let me die rather than to know the mortification of surrender."

Mrs. Motte turned to the young officer. "Captain," she said, "it is not dishonor. Think of surrender as I did of burning my home—that is one of the fortunes of war."

Thus, Mrs. Motte gained the respect of the British as well as the Americans. In fact, all who knew her found her kind and charitable.

Later it was said that Mrs. Motte kept her knitting needles in the quiver where the arrows were once stored.

When she died in 1815, she was buried in Old Philip's Church, which burned long ago. Another church now stands on the same site.

Dorcas Nelson Richardson

FAITHFUL WIFE
1741–1834

Dorcas Nelson of the Sumter District was the daughter of Captain John Nelson, a native of Ireland who married a Miss Brownson of South Carolina. For many years the Nelson family operated Nelson's Ferry over the Santee River.

Dorcas married Richard Richardson and moved farther up the river near the junction of the Congaree and Wateree rivers.

When the Revolutionary War began, Richard became captain of a company of militia. At the surrender of Charleston, he was taken prisoner and sent to Johns Island, where he contracted smallpox. The British failed to observe the conditions on which he had surrendered; consequently, as soon as he recovered, he escaped and hid in the dark thickets of the Santee Swamp near his home.

During this time Colonel Banastre Tarleton and his British troops had made the Richardson home a station for their calvary. The British soldiers restricted Dorcas and her children to several rooms of their home and allowed them only a scanty share of their own food.

Every day Mrs. Richardson sent her husband a portion of her allowance by a Negro servant. She also sent his favorite riding horse into the swamp so that it would not, along with the other animals, fall into the enemy's hands.

Sometimes Mrs. Richardson even ventured to visit her husband on the small knoll in the heart of the swamp. It is said that their initials carved into the bark of trees can still be seen there.

It was not long, however, before the British learned of Richardson's escape. Scouts were sent in every direction and a reward offered for his capture.

Frequently the British officers boasted to Dorcas of what they would do to her husband when they captured him.

"We'll hang him" one jeered, "on that walnut tree right by your door, and you'll get to see him kick."

"I do not doubt," Dorcas answered with calmness, "that men who can threaten a woman would be capable of just such an act of inhumanity toward a brave enemy. But capture him before you boast."

On one occasion some of the officers showed Mrs. Richardson swords covered with blood and told her it was the blood of her husband. Another time they told her he had been hanged.

One day when the British troops were on an expedition, Richardson appeared at his home. The happy reunion was cut short, however, when a patrolling party of the British appeared unexpectedly.

Mrs. Richardson dashed to the door as the soldiers were about to enter and pretended to be intently busy about something at the front door. Thus, she blocked their entrance until her husband could slip through the back and to the swamp again.

Before long, Richardson had joined General Francis Marion. When the British heard this, they changed their manner of dealing with Dorcas. Instead of denouncing her husband as before, they now professed a respect for him.

"The British could use the services of such a man," they said. "You should prevail upon your husband to join the Royal Army. It would mean wealth and honorable promotion."

"I have nothing but contempt for you," the spirited woman answered, "and I will never be an instrument for your purpose."

Furthermore, Dorcas sent a message to her husband assuring him that she and the children were well and he must never join the British for the sake of their welfare.

It was such calm judgment and strength of mind that sustained Dorcas Nelson Richardson, as well as her husband and children, in the trials during the Revolutionary War. Throughout her long life (she died at the age of ninety-three), she maintained a disposition of unusual serenity and cheerfulness.

Sarah Reeve Gibbes

GUARDIAN
1746–1825

The brick mansion, with its broad portico facing the Stono River on Johns Island, stood under an umbrella of oak, aspen, and sycamore. Nearby, a battalion of British soldiers moved stealthily in the predawn light. They would make this inviting home, called Peaceful Retreat, their headquarters.

Inside, an aged servant tapped softly at Mrs. Gibbes' door.

Charleston Harbor in 1780

"Missus," he whispered, "the Redcoats are all 'round the house."

"Tell no one, Caesar." Her voice was soft and calm. "Keep all quiet."

Sarah dressed quickly, awakened several ladies who were guests in the house, and requested they dress.

In the meantime, still moving quietly, she directed the servants to prepare the children—her own eight and eight others left in her care by deceased relatives. The oldest child was fifteen.

Sarah assisted her husband, who was crippled by rheumatism, to his wheel chair.

All was done so silently that the British had no idea anyone was yet awake in the house.

At daylight the vigilant British heard the heavy rolling of Mr. Gibbes' wheel chair across the spacious hall to the front door. Supposing the sound to be the rolling of a cannon, they advanced and stood with pointed bayonets.

A soldier flung open the door, only to find the stately form of an invalid surrounded by women and children.

Mrs. Gibbes addressed the group in her calm manner that demanded respect. In spite of the soldiers' pillaging, Sarah Gibbes kept her place as mistress of the household and treated her uninvited guests with dignity.

Later when vessels from Charleston arrived to dislodge the enemy, Mrs. Gibbes walked miles in drizzling rain to take the children to an adjoining plantation. Wet, chilled, and exhausted, the group had stopped for a brief rest at a laborer's home when she realized her nephew, little John Fenwick, was missing. In their hurry and terror, they had left him behind. What was to be done now? The servants who had accompanied her refused to risk their lives by returning for him. The roar of guns in the distant night was frightening enough.

Mary Anna, Mrs. Gibbes' thirteen-year-old daughter, spoke up. "Mother, I will return for John."

Fear stabbed at Sarah Gibbes' heart. How could she let her go? And yet, she could not refuse her noble offer.

With her mother's blessing, Mary Anna hastened along the dark path with all the speed she could muster.

When she reached their home, she found it still in possession of the British, who at first refused her entrance.

Finally, she gained permission and dashed searching through the house. In a third-floor bedroom she found her little cousin cowering in a corner. Mary Anna gathered him in her arms and fled into the night. Shots fell about them as they ran to join the others.

With the children safe from the shelling of the area, Mrs. Gibbes returned home to be with her husband.

Susannah Smith Elliott

FLAG MAKER
CIRCA 1750–(?)

The time was June 28, 1776. Gulls circled and swooped over the Atlantic shoreline. Warm sea breezes stirred the marsh grass of the creeks.

Richard Taylor

The blue Second Regiment flag made by Susannah Elliott

At Fort Moultrie on Sullivan's Island a young bride, Susannah Elliott, stood before the Second South Carolina Regiment. Three days earlier these men had gallantly defended their fort against the British. In her hand Susannah held two elegant silk flags which she had embroidered. One was red; the other, dark blue.

While her proud husband, Colonel Barnard Elliott, looked on, Susannah proclaimed, "Your gallant behavior in defense of liberty and your country entitles you to the highest honors. I make not the least doubt, under Heaven's protection, you will stand by these colors as long as they wave in the air of liberty."

Touched by her faith in them, the soldiers made a promise that the flags should be "honorably supported and never tarnished."

This promise of the Second Regiment was literally kept. At Savannah several soldiers lost their lives attempting to plant the flag on the British lines.

Sergeant William Jasper, who had been honored earlier for rescuing the blue flag with a silver crescent in the battle of Fort Moultrie, was one of the soldiers to receive a mortal wound in attempting to plant the flag at Savannah. Just before his retreat from battle, dying Jasper said, "Tell Mrs. Elliott I lost my life supporting the colors she presented to our regiment."

It is said that the flags were afterward taken at the fall of Charleston and deposited in the Tower of London. Susannah's blue banner was traced to the Royal Green Jackets' regimental museum, and in 1970 it was returned to South Carolina on loan.

A variety of flags were carried by the Patriots during the Revolutionary War, as our United States flag was not adopted until June 14, 1777.

Eliza Yonge Wilkinson

WOMAN OF LETTERS
1757–(?)

Cherokee rose hedged the Wilkinson home on Yonge's Island. A short distance away a boat moved along the Stono River. The scene could have been one of serenity had not the boat been occupied by Red Coats.

Eliza Yonge Wilkinson, daughter of Francis and Sarah Clifford Yonge, kept a diary during these turbulent times. On one occasion she wrote of the British riding up to her home in such a fury that their horses kicked up sod.

"Where are these women rebels I've heard about?" a soldier called out.

With swords drawn and pistols cocked, they jerked off the ruffled caps of the women, grabbing the jeweled pins from them. They plundered their homes, splitting trunks for quick access to the contents.

"Please—" Eliza addressed a ruffian who had her clothes thrown over his arm. "In such times I cannot replace my clothing. At least let me keep a change."

His response came in a curse as he knelt to cut the buckles from her shoes.

A soldier who accompanied him screamed, "Shares! I want one of them buckles."

Near Eliza a friend begged to be allowed to keep her wedding ring, but facing a cocked pistol she gave it up.

"Thank your stars," the retreating soldiers told them, "that we favored you. It could have been worse."

Later, when some Whig troops came by with British prisoners, two were the very ones who had treated Eliza and her friends so cruelly. Seeing the soldiers with their hands tied behind them, Eliza felt pity and held water to their lips.

Toward the end of the war, Mrs. Wilkinson visited some friends on a prison ship, where she spoke out against the British. She also refused a Britisher's request to play the guitar.

"I will not play, Sir," she retorted, "until my countrymen return."

"Return as what, Madam, prisoners or subjects?"

"As conquerers, Sir!"

The soldier laughed. "You will never see that, Madam!"

Like many others, Mrs. Wilkinson also refused to take part in the amusements of Charleston while it was in possession of the British. When news came of the victory of General Washington over Cornwallis, she was at her home on Yonge's Island.

Other than keeping a diary, Mrs. Wilkinson wrote numerous letters to friends and especially to Mary Porcher. In these letters, as well as in her diary, she recalled the invasion of South Carolina and the taking of Charleston by the British in 1779. At a later date Caroline Gilman collected and edited these letters for publication in her magazine, *Southern Rose Bud*, and eventually in book form as *Letters of Eliza Wilkinson*. Other unpublished letters and poetry present a picture of Charleston and plantation society.

After the death of Eliza's first husband, Joseph Wilkinson, she married Peter Porcher, Sr., of Saint Peter's Parish. They had one son, Francis Yonge Porcher.

The old family mansion on the island no longer exists, but the burial ground is still sacred.

Grace and Rachel Martin

PATRIOTS

Grace and Rachel Martin remained at home in Ninety Six District with their mother-in-law while their husbands fought in the Revolutionary War.

One evening, news reached them that a courier bearing an important message to an upper station would pass along their road. The courier would be guarded by two British officers.

The young women decided to waylay the party and obtain possession of the papers.

Grace and Rachel quickly disguised themselves in their husbands' clothing, took guns, and in the darkness of the night stationed themselves at a point beside the road where they knew the escort must pass.

The silence of the shadowy night was soon broken by the tramp of horses.

As the courier and his guards appeared, the disguised women leaped from their hiding places and at gunpoint demanded the surrender of the dispatches.

Taken by surprise, the men promptly yielded.

A trusted Colonial messenger hurried the confiscated message to Nathanael Greene, and the girls darted home by a short cut.

The officers, thwarted in their mission, turned back down the road along which they had come. Oddly enough, they stopped at the home of Mrs. Martin and her daughters-in-law, Grace and Rachel, to ask for accommodations as weary travelers.

"But," Mrs. Martin questioned, "you passed here a short while ago, did you not?"

"We were accosted by two rebel lads," answered the courier, "and our mission has been defeated."

"Had you no arms?" Mrs. Martin asked.

"Yes, but we were taken so suddenly we had no time to use our weapons."

The next morning the men departed, never suspecting they had been overpowered by the very women whose hospitality they had accepted.

Laodicea Langston Springfield

WHIG MESSENGER
CIRCA 1760

"Dicey," her father instructed, "you are not to warn anyone else of the Tories' plans—no matter what you hear. We are in enough trouble already living in the midst of people on both sides of the Revolution. Don't anger them further."

Dicey's forehead wrinkled over her black eyes. At least her father, Samuel Langston, had not been angry enough with her to use her full name. "But, what about James, Father?" she asked. "What if—?"

"No, not even your brother."

Frustration flooded Dicey. She had just returned from a visit with a friend whose family had gone over to the British side. While there, she had overheard talk about a surprise attack the next day. Now that Charles Town had fallen, banks of outlaws and bandits had aligned themselves with the Tories against the Patriots. It was these desperadoes, who were out to plunder under the protection of the British law, that Dicey needed to warn her Patriot brother and his men against.

Dicey didn't want to disobey her father. "If he were not old and feeble," she told herself, "he would want me to warn James and the Elder Settlement that the Tories are going to attack." Anyway, if her mother were living, she would want her to save her brother's life. She had no choice.

At dark, Dicey set out on foot under a western Carolina moon. To saddle a horse and ride out among the Tories would arouse curiosity. She had to walk as fast as she could. The woods looked different to her at night. Ghostly shadows moved across her path. She fought feelings of panic. Twigs cracked around her, and night animals made eerie sounds.

Now and then she came out of the woods to cross a field or skirt a marsh before going into the darkness of another wooded area. Several times she had to cross streams swollen by recent rains.

Finally, she reached the banks of the rising Tyger River. The water rushed and tumbled at her feet. Could she make it? What if the current of the cold, dark river swept her away?

If so, James and the others would die at the hands of the Tories. Clenching her teeth, Dicey stepped into the water. She could scarcely keep her feet on the bottom as the current pulled her about. In mid-channel the water came up to her neck, swirling her in a dizzying circle before sweeping her onto the opposite shore.

Wet and shivering, she made it to the lean-to where James and his friends were. "Quickly," she warned, "send your men in all directions to tell the neighbors—the Bloody Scouts are coming!"

Before her, James' face showed his weariness. "The truth of it is, Sister, my men are faint with hunger and want of sleep, for we have just returned from an expedition."

"Then build a fire," Dicey commanded, "and I'll bake them a hoecake."

James could not help admiring his spunky little sister. "You're as wet as a rat and have booted it over many miles of Carolina woods. 'Tis a sad thing you must cook for us."

In moments Dicey had sparked a fire with planks ripped from the place where they'd found shelter. Soon she was stuffing the hot bread into the men's saddle bags. "You can eat on the way," she said.

Thanks to Dicey's warning, the men escaped and the people of the Elder Settlement, or Little Eden, received warning.

The next morning Dicey made breakfast for her father just as if she had not been away.

On another occasion, after the Tories lost a fight with Patriots—who happened to have a Langston lad among them—they descended upon the Langston household. Dicey was helping to lay out apples to dry when she heard the tramping of the horses.

By the time she reached the parlor, one of the tormentors was holding her gray-haired father against the wall with a pistol pointed at his chest. Dicey rushed across the room and flung her arms around her father's neck.

"Get out of the way, girl," a soldier shouted, "unless you want to be shot with this old traitor!"

"Shoot me if you dare!" Dicey shrieked. "But do not shoot a helpless old man, you coward."

"The girl has spunk," one of the other Tories said. "Let the old man go."

The soldier cursed and lowered his gun. Still muttering oaths, they turned their horses and galloped away.

Another time Dicey was determined to keep her brother's trust. He had left a rifle in her care, telling her the courier would identify himself with a countersign.

When a group of soldiers commanded by young Thomas Springfield arrived and asked for the rifle, Dicey immediately ran for the gun. Upon returning with it, she remembered she had forgotten to ask for the sign. She stopped short and made her demand.

"You are too late, Miss Laodicea," said young Springfield, stepping forward. "You and the gun are now in our power." He flashed her a handsome smile and reached for the gun.

Dicey cocked the rifle and leveled it toward his head. "Oh, are we?" she asked. "Then come and get us."

Thomas Springfield promptly gave the countersign against a background of laughter from his men.

After the war ended, Dicey became Mrs. Thomas Springfield. The couple established a home near Travelers Rest. There Dicey, surrounded by her children and grandchildren, lived for many years.

Emily Geiger

COURIER
CIRCA 1760–(?)

General Nathanael Greene paced the length of his tent in the temporary camp at the fork of the Enoree and Broad rivers in Newberry County. It was June 1781, and he had just retreated from Ninety Six after his month-long siege against Star Fort, an effort thwarted by the arrival of Lord Rawdon and his troops.

Even though his assault on the fort had failed, General Greene was not willing to give up. The enemy was weaker now. If only he could strike one more blow!

Generals Thomas Sumter and Francis Marion, who were in the Low Country, had planned to join him, but it would be suicidal for their troops to attempt a union now. They would be running right into the hands of the Redcoats, for

Richard Taylor

The arrest of Emily Geiger

Lord Rawdon would continue to pursue them until they crossed the Enoree.

If only he could get a dispatch to Sumter on the Wateree River telling him where they could meet. But the idea was unthinkable. His soldiers were battle weary. No one was willing to take a message through the Tory-infested midlands. It would be asking for death.

At that moment a guard appeared at his tent opening. "Excuse me, Sir. There is a young country girl to see you."

Greene turned, the worry lines on his face changing to consternation. "A young lady? What would a woman be doing here?"

"Yes, Sir—she said something about delivering a message."

"Send her in."

Momentarily a young woman dressed in a dark riding habit gave a quick curtsy before General Greene. Her breath came in short gasps, and she fidgeted with the small riding whip in her hand. A deep flush came over her face as she said, "I have been told, General, that you are in want of a bearer of dispatches to General Sumter."

"Yes," the General answered, "but as yet I have found no one bold enough to undertake the mission."

"Send me," she said, her eyes alight and brown curls dancing.

"Send *you*? Why, I could not do that, my child. It is a journey from which brave men hold back."

"Give me a fleet horse, and I will bear your message safely."

A hint of a smile began to spread across the General's face before he asked:

"How old are you, my child?"

"Eighteen, Sir."

"Is your father living?"

"Yes, Sir. He is a planter who lives not two miles from here. But he is an invalid and unable to bear arms with you."

"Have you his consent?"

"He knows nothing of my intention, but he loves his country as I do, Sir. I am sure his head would approve though his heart might fail him if I were to ask his consent."

"Your offer is heroic but the risk of danger is too high." For a second General Greene was lost in thought, and then he turned to face the young girl. He could not deny that a girl could probably make it past the British soldiers whereas one of his men could not.

"Would you go alone?" he asked.

"Yes. Alone, Sir."

"What is your name, Child?"

"Emily Geiger, Sir."

"Noble girl, you shall go," the General said. "May God speed and protect you."

"He will," Emily murmured.

General Greene ordered a swift, well-trained horse to be saddled while he wrote the dispatch to General Sumter.

After receiving instructions, Emily slipped the folded parchment into the bodice of her dress and prepared to leave.

Whispers had circulated through the camp, and officers and men gathered to see the brave girl begin her perilous journey.

Without fear, Emily placed her foot in the cupped palm of an officer and sprang into the saddle.

General Greene put his left hand on the flank of her horse. "If you are arrested," he said, "destroy the message as quickly as you can."

Grasping her right hand, he added, "May heaven and your country reward you." He pressed his lips to her hand and turned toward his tent.

The officer let go of the bridle. Emily dug her heels into her horse and galloped away.

The long, lonely road moved beneath them as her strong horse plunged forward, leaving swirls of dust between the rider and the silent soldiers.

Late in the afternoon Emily passed Morgan's Range and followed a bridle path toward the Saluda River above its junction with the Broad River. She could cross the Congaree just below the junction of the two rivers and then go as directly as possible to General Sumter's camp on the Wateree River.

The shadows of evening fell over Emily and her weary horse. The house where she had expected to stop was still miles away.

Fearing she might lose her way in the darkness, she decided to stop at the first farmhouse she might come across.

Before long, Emily stood before a cabin door to be greeted kindly by a man who asked where she was going.

"I did hope," said Emily, "to reach Elwoods' tonight. How far is it?"

"Over ten miles and the road is bad and lonely. You'd better stay with us."

Emily dismounted. The man led her horse to the stable while his wife invited her inside.

"Have you come far?" She looked earnestly into Emily's face.

Emily hesitated. Was she with friends or enemies?

The woman continued. "Your horse looks very tired. You must have ridden a long distance."

"I rode fast," Emily offered.

"It is hardly safe for a woman to take such a journey alone in these times."

"I am not afraid."

"But, Child, it was only a day or so ago since Greene was in retreat. It may be that some of his rag-a-muffins are still about."

A chill passed over Emily. This couple was not a friend to the Whig cause—nor to her.

"What is your name?" the woman asked.

Again Emily hesitated before she replied, "Geiger."

"Not John Geiger's daughter!"

"Yes."

The woman turned to her husband who was entering the room. "Would you believe it? This girl is the daughter of John Geiger we have heard so much about."

The man looked at Emily. "No wonder your horse is tired," he said, "if you've ridden that far, and no doubt you are hungry, too."

He raised his hand to the questioning look on his wife's face. "Let's have supper. She should have food and shelter even if she were the daughter of my worst enemy."

After the meal Emily was allowed to retire. Alone, she wondered what she should do. But before she knew it, she had fallen into a deep sleep.

Sometime in the night she was awakened by the sound of horses' hoofs nearing the house.

A voice called out familiarly: "Hello, there, Preston. I may be on a fool's errand, but have you seen anything of a stray woman in these parts?"

The shutters of Emily's room were open to the night air. She eased toward the window to see a rider dismount and enter the house. For a long time afterward she heard the murmur of voices.

"It must be their intention to wait until morning to capture me," she thought. "I must get away."

Finally, when the house was still, Emily climbed from her window and into the feeble moonlight. The great head of a dog met her. She patted him and he wagged his tail.

Once in the stable, she searched for her horse. She found a bridle and—without a saddle—mounted and galloped off.

Near daylight Emily reached the home of her friend and poured forth her

Emily Geiger tears up and swallows the message.

South Caroliniana Library

story. He provided her with a fresh horse and she swept away once more on her mission before the sun rose.

Emily had just crossed Friday's Ferry on the Congaree when her heart gave a leap. Three uniformed men came into view directly in front of her. They had seen her. It would be of no use to turn back. She rode on, trying to be brave.

One of the soldiers pulled away from the others. With one hand outstretched, he motioned for her to stop. In the other, he held a musket.

"You were right," he called over his shoulder to his companion. "It's a girl." Then looking at Emily he asked rather rudely, "And why, pray tell, is a young woman like you out riding alone on such a dismal road?"

"I like riding alone. If you think I'm here for any other reason, then bring a woman to search me."

One soldier reached for her bridal reins, another for her satchel.

Soon she was being questioned before Lord Rawdon. Not wanting to lie, Emily gave evasive answers.

Shortly, she found herself locked in a deserted cabin. She knew a British scout had sent for a Tory matron to search her. With trembling fingers, Emily slipped the note from her dress bodice and read it carefully. Then she closed her eyes and repeated the message. There was no need to try to hide it. They would search the room too.

Turning her back to the door, Emily tore the dispatch into small pieces, chewed them, and swallowed.

When the soldier returned with the woman to search Emily, she found nothing. Emily was released.

Knowing she might be followed, Emily returned to the home of her Patriot friend. He gave her a guide to point out an old Indian trail that would skirt the point where Sumter was encamped. They rode all night.

At sunrise when the guide turned back, Emily did not stop to rest herself or her horse but pressed on as the sun became hotter and hotter.

In the late afternoon, faint and weary and sick with hunger, she recognized the tent rows of Sumter's small camp.

So tired she could hardly speak, Emily demanded of the sentinel, "Take me to General Sumter. I have a message from General Greene."

Before Sumter, she repeated word for word the contents of the dispatch she had destroyed.

General Sumter never doubted her word. He gave an immediate command and in an hour he had assembled his band. The drums rattled and the clarions blew. Sumter's soldiers were on the march toward Orangeburg to join General Greene.

After the Revolutionary War ended, Emily Geiger married a planter named Threrwitz and lived near Granby, South Carolina. When she died, she was buried in Threrwitz Cemetery in Lexington County.

One of the greatest honors bestowed upon Emily Geiger Threrwitz occurred when South Carolina made a new seal to replace the one made after the British were defeated on Sullivan's Island. It was suggested that the woman holding the branch of laurel be designated as Emily Geiger.

Maria Martin

NATURALIST–ARTIST
1796–1863

John James Audubon stood back to admire the painting on the easel before him. "Ah, Maria!" he exclaimed, "I can always rely on you to add just the right elements."

Maria Martin glowed with pleasure at having pleased her friend, for Audubon was renowned for his paintings of American birds. In fact, Audubon was the first person to encourage Maria in her artistic talents.

With deft strokes she painted leaves, twigs, flowers and butterflies. She might draw blossoms, a wriggling caterpillar, or a moth in flight. Whatever was needed for a background for Audubon's birds, whether it be a catkin or a floret, Maria painted. According to custom, Audubon painted the bird first, placing it on a short, unadorned branch or twig and filling in the background himself or

Richard Taylor

Maria Martin painted backgrounds for Audubon's birds.

leaving it for his assistants to complete.

"The insects you draw," declared Audubon, "are perhaps the best I have ever seen." Often, too, Audubon praised Maria for her color and balance.

Maria also contributed to the works of others: she helped her brother-in-law, the Reverend John Bachman, with his plant collecting and provided accurate pictures of reptiles for John Edwards Holbrook, a leading zoologist.

With several outstanding gardens of Charleston for observation, she sketched from growing plants. Thus, her backgrounds combine scientific precision with an artist's feeling for composition, color, and design.

Because Maria's sister Harriet, the wife of John Bachman, was weak from bearing fourteen children, Maria shouldered much of the domestic responsibility in their Charleston home. She also helped her brother-in-law with his work as a clergyman and welcomed visitors to the Rutledge Avenue home. One of these visitors was the noted John James Audubon. Under Audubon's constant praise, Maria collected, studied, and made exacting renderings of moths, caterpillars, butterflies, and other insects. She also served as editor and critic for Audubon's *Quadrupeds of America*.

In 1848, two years after the death of her sister, Maria married Bachman.

A patriotic Southerner, Maria Martin Bachman was active in the support of the Southern cause during the gathering storm before the Civil War. When her health began to fail, Bachman sent her and several of his children and grandchildren to a house he owned in Columbia. She spent part of her latter years writing verse for children.

Maria Martin Bachman died in 1863 in Columbia. Thus, she was spared the knowledge that her home was later burned to the ground by Sherman's men.

Even though Maria received no public recognition during her lifetime, she made a place for herself as America's first woman naturalist-artist. Several museums and galleries have displayed her watercolors and drawings. Even some "Audubon" paintings are said to be hers.

If Maria Martin, Charlestonian and granddaughter of a Lutheran minister, had tried to make a name for herself, she would probably have failed. At that time in history, women competing in the arts and sciences was frowned upon. Instead, she achieved fulfillment by giving her loving work to others.

CIVIL WAR TIMES

The Civil War period was a particularly difficult time for the women of South Carolina. Since most of the fighting was on Southern ground, women of the South were often caught up in the struggle. There naturally followed many acts of bravery and courage.

Although South Carolina women were generally staunch supporters of the Southern cause, some among them had strong feelings about slavery. Because of this inner conflict, the time leading up to the war was an extremely emotional one.

Fortunately, some women recorded their day-to-day trials in their diaries, thus preserving feelings, times, places, and events in history.

Others put "self" in the background and threw themselves wholeheartedly into the war effort, devoting countless hours to the cause. They made clothing for volunteers in the Confederate Army and cared for wounded soldiers. At the same time they struggled—with heads held high in determination—to keep their homes together.

Still other women felt the need to protect and preserve traditions of the South. Many cities, towns, plantations, and historical landmarks lay in ruins. Singly and together women worked—often at great sacrifice—to restore their beloved South.

During this period, too, women began to speak out for their rights as individuals and as citizens.

It is to all of these women and others whom history does not record that our state owes a great debt of gratitude.

Sarah Moore Grimké

1792–1873

Angelina Emily Grimké

1805–1879
ABOLITIONISTS

"Oh, Mother, please—" Sarah begged.

"Now, Sarah, be reasonable." Mrs. Grimké's voice reflected weakness from having just given birth to her fourteenth child. "How can you be your sister's godmother when you are not even thirteen?"

"Oh, but I can. I can, Mother." Sarah turned toward her father standing at the head of her mother's bed. "Father—God will help me. I know he will."

The usually stern expression of Judge John Faucheraud Grimké, a wealthy planter and slaveholder and distinguished leader of Charleston, became soft for a moment. "The child will grow up to be just like Sarah," he said.

A few weeks later Sarah Moore Grimké became the godmother of her sister Angelina Emily in a christening ceremony at Saint Philip's Church in Charleston.

The new baby became the hope of Sarah's life. She called her "Precious Nina," and little Nina called Sarah "Mother."

Mauma, the old Negro in charge of the nursemaids and a woman of great kindness, did not have to worry about the care of Angelina. Sarah kept her vow made as godmother.

Not being allowed to study her brother Thomas's books had caused Sarah much heartache. Even Thomas had deserted her when she pleaded with her father to let her study Latin.

Upon receiving dolls and satin slippers for gifts rather than books as did her brothers, Sarah would cry in desperation, "Oh, why did I have to be born a girl?"

In truth she would have made a more suitable boy, for her rugged good health in a world that prized female delicacy seemed out of character. Too, her long straight nose and firm jaw looked awkward framed by curls and a bonnet.

Shocked over the behavior of his daughter, her father once remarked, "Yes, it is too bad, Sarah, that you were not a boy. You would have made an excellent lawyer as you like to argue."

Sarah found, too, that her mother, whose ancestors were colonial governors, was often upset because her daughter was so hardheaded. And Sarah's mother could not understand why Sarah liked to daydream about the ships docked in the harbor.

"All a Southern lady needs to know," Mary Grimké would say, "is a little needlework, a little music, a little dancing, and perhaps a little French; otherwise, she might strain her feminine mind."

But Sarah yearned for knowledge of mathematics, the natural sciences, and Greek.

It exasperated her even more when her mother said, "Do try to be a polite lady like your sisters, and you will have no worry finding a husband. You are from the right family."

Sarah knew this was her mother's polite way of saying her daughter was far from pretty.

Nevertheless, all this talk was as boring to Sarah as the parties she attended while she was growing up. Although she liked the part of the year in which the family stayed in Charleston better than the part spent on the plantation, she did not care for the party life there. Often she would leave the ballroom early and write in her diary. It was during such times that Sarah felt great sadness that she was not using the talents God had given her.

For a short while she taught classes for slave children. After seeing their eagerness to learn to read, she began to tutor some in private.

When Judge Grimké discovered her teaching, he was quick to cut it short. "Reading only makes slaves restless and rebellious. Besides, teaching slaves to read is strictly against the law."

Sarah could hardly believe what she had heard. Yet it was true. Her father took a law book from his library shelf and showed her the 1740 Act, which said slaves were not to be taught to read or write.

Richard Taylor

Angelina Emily Grimké   *Sarah Moore Grimké*

Another great sadness came into Sarah's life when she became aware of other cruel aspects of slavery. She could not understand how persons who attended church and professed to be Christians could treat their slaves so cruelly, even resorting to such torturing devices as heavy iron collars with prongs to prevent slaves from resting or straps tied from a lifted ankle to the neck. Families who could not bear to punish their own slaves sent them to workhouses set up for that purpose.

The only truly bright spot in Sarah's life was little Angelina. One day, however, Nina fainted at school and had to be brought home.

Alone with Sarah, Angelina sobbed out what she had witnessed. A little slave boy who belonged to one of the children in her class had been sent to open a window when she noticed he could barely walk. Open wounds bled down the back of his legs.

Sarah had no answers for her little sister, but they wept together. Judge Grimké's prediction had come true: The sisters were of one heart and mind.

While Mrs. Grimké worried that her daughter would be an old maid, Sarah herself became more and more dissatisfied with the life of a Southern belle. She tried to keep herself occupied by helping Nina with her lessons, her mother with the household, and taking part in church.

When Judge Grimké became ill, it was Sarah who accompanied him to consult a doctor in Philadelphia. She sat by her father many long hours before death came.

On her way home to South Carolina, Sarah was befriended by a group of Quakers. In her loneliness and confusion she was overjoyed to find that the Quakers shared some of her views, particularly about slavery.

Eventually Sarah came to realize that she did not fit into the Southern way of life and decided to move to Philadelphia and become a Quaker.

Telling her mother "I am sorry that I have caused you great pain and embarrassment, I love you, and I appreciate your willingness to let me go," Sarah left Charleston.

Angelina had grown into a pampered, popular girl of eighteen. Still, through Sarah's influence she had a mind of her own. Angelina shocked everyone by going before the officials of the Church and asking them to speak out against slavery. They refused.

More and more the Charleston customs became too much for her to bear. "Why," she questioned her mother, "must we continually order slaves up and down the stairs to open windows and fetch us a cup of tea?"

On another occasion she burst into tears when her brother John whipped his slave. Finally, she sailed north to join Sarah.

The Quaker village, with its quaint brick houses and housewives in simple black dresses, was like stepping into another world. Here men lived by the sweat of their brows. There were Negroes, but they were free. Angelina saw a dignity about them as they sold their wares in the street.

But much to the Grimké sisters' sorrow, they observed prejudice within the Quaker meetings. Although the Quakers spoke against slavery, they practiced segregation.

Faced with this new frustration, Sarah and Angelina did the only thing they knew to do—they appealed to the women of the South to help them overthrow slavery. For the first time Southern women addressed other Southern women about the evils of slavery.

The sisters were called "female agitators" by people who said they had brought shame and dishonor to their "fair sex." Thus, the fight for slavery moved into the fight for equal rights for women.

Sarah and Angelina were called on to speak in public places throughout the Northeast, something most unusual in their day. All over New England women flocked to hear them speak. Many of them walked miles and against their husbands' orders. Sometimes male hecklers tried to break up the lectures, and some places barred their use of auditoriums. Nevertheless, the sisters continued until they won the right for respectable women to speak in public.

"Why," they asked, "did God give brains to both men and women if only men are allowed to use them?"

A few men were on their sides, but they wanted the sisters to speak *only* on the slavery situation, not on women.

One of these men was Theodore Weld, a tall, thin man who looked stern until he spoke; then his kindness and warmth shone through. Before meeting the Grimkés, he had chosen abolition as his ministry, sacrificing his health for the cause. He lectured so much his voice became barely a whisper, and because of repeated abuse upon him, he became known as "the most mobbed man in the United States." Although Weld pledged not to marry until slavery was abolished, he and Angelina began a correspondence that ended in marriage.

Before a black minister and both black and white friends, the two spoke vows they had written—vows promising equality of men and women of all races before God.

Sarah came to live with the married couple, serving as nursemaid to their children. The three adults continued their interest in the cause of slavery. They worked with the Beechers, William Lloyd Garrison, and other leaders of the abolition movement. The sisters also remained leaders for women's rights. They even wore publicly a Bloomer costume, a short skirt worn over trousers fastened at the ankles. This attire did away with the tight stays, bustles, and layers of petticoats women had always worn. Thus, the costume became a symbol of women's liberation.

When the Civil War began, Sarah and Angelina committed themselves fully to the Northern cause.

Upon the deaths of the Grimké sisters, the very newspapers that had attacked them for their rebelliousness praised them as pioneers in the fight for slavery and women's rights.

Louisa Cheves McCord

AUTHOR–NURSE
1810–1879

Louisa set another of the great bowls of steaming stew on the long table on her back porch. Close by, her daughters placed platters heaped with cornbread.

From buildings on the campus of South Carolina College across the street, convalescing soldiers dragged themselves to her tempting dishes. For those unable to walk, Louisa hurried food to the temporary military hospital set up at the college. There she lingered to help the sick.

The happy years of Louisa's life were gone: her husband, Colonel David James McCord, had died; her son Langdon had gone to Virginia to fight the Yankees. Louisa had left her beloved plantation, Lang Syne on the Congaree River, in care of an overseer and moved to her town house in Columbia. Now that the war had begun, there was no time for the writing and translating she had enjoyed in the past.

All of her time was taken up by the Soldiers' Relief and Ladies' Clothing associations in the city of Columbia. Her life belonged to the boys in gray. Even a moment's break in her nursing duties as director of the Confederate Hospital on the present University of South Carolina campus was devoted to knitting socks.

The McCord home at Pendleton and Bull streets, built by her husband, became part of the overflowing hospital complex and a collection point for food.

Back at Lang Syne, Louisa had the Negroes bring out old spinning wheels to make cloth. She cut up her carpets to make blankets for the soldiers. She melted her lead pipes to make bullets. Besides all this, Louisa gave her horses to the Confederate Army and sent her plantation people to work on trenches and fortifications.

While nursing wounded soldiers, Louisa learned that her own son had been killed at the second battle of Bull Run.

On February 17, 1865, Federal forces occupied Columbia. Louisa's home became headquarters for General O.O. Howard, second in command under Sherman. Thus, her home escaped burning. Her diary records this period.

One morning she and her daughters found a note from a Federal soldier. "Ladies," it said, "I pity you; leave this town—go anywhere to be safer than here." It had been scribbled on a torn leaf from her dead son's notebook.

But Louisa did not leave. Already her private papers had been destroyed and scattered. Running away would mean the end of everything.

That night homes all over Columbia were looted and burned. In the morning two-thirds of the city lay in smoldering ruins.

As the head of a delegation of Columbia women, Louisa took a request to General Howard in her own home. The request asked that the people might

Sandlapper Magazine

be told what they could expect for the second night.

General William T. Sherman was with Howard as he turned and said, "You may rest assured, Mrs. McCord, that nothing like what happened last night will happen again."

The McCord home in which the conversation took place is listed in the National Register of Historic Places.

Always dedicated to her beliefs, Louisa spoke out in her earlier years for women's rights in her essays "Enfranchisement of Women" and "Woman and Her Needs." Characterized by sharp logic, her writings were regularly accepted by *DeBow's Review* and *The Southern Quarterly Review,* two influential journals of the ante-bellum period.

Louisa lived out her life with her daughter, Louisa McCord Smythe, in

Charleston. Upon her death on November 23, 1879, she was buried in Charleston's Magnolia Cemetery.

Louisa Cheves McCord was the daughter of Langdon Cheves of Charleston, a noted statesman and friend of John C. Calhoun. The Cheves' plantation, Lang Syne, was later owned by Julia Peterkin, the South Carolina author who wrote stories about many of the descendants of the McCords' former slaves.

Ann Pamela Cunningham

PRESERVER OF MOUNT VERNON
1816–1875

Seventeen-year-old Pamela tugged at the shawl around her slim shoulders and smoothed her bright red hair back against her pillows.

Outside her room off the long hallway of Rosemont Plantation, she could hear faintly the voices of her mother's distinguished visitors.

"It must be terribly hard for Ann Pamela to be confined with her back problem."

And then their voices fell almost to a whisper, for well-educated people of her day always refrained from discussing openly such delicate subjects as the nature of one's illness.

"Actually," she heard her mother say, "she does quite well to have been so active. She enjoys her governess and she is an avid reader, you know. Her mind is always busy."

The voices faded away as the ladies moved down the long flight of stairs. For a moment Pamela's mind drifted back to the days when she rode horseback over the broad grounds of their plantation near Laurens. Her grandfather, Patrick Cunningham, had built the house about a hundred years before she was born on the ninety-thousand-acre tract of land given to him by the king of England. Pamela's parents, Louisa Bird and Robert Cunningham, quartered 500 servants on the estate. Seven spectacular gardens surrounded the house.

"I can recognize you from far off," her father had teased, "for no other rider has such a mop of red hair flailing behind."

It was true that Pamela's delicate frame of barely five feet did make her appear to be all head from a distance. But during her teen years the delicate limbs and body expanded and rounded into lovely womanhood.

After being tutored at home, Pamela found her years at Barhamville Academy in Columbia happy ones, for she was always eager to learn.

Growing up as an only daughter who has everything could have spoiled Pamela, but friends at the school found her to be not only "quite pretty with her bluish gray eyes and lovely complexion, but intelligent, cordial, and mannerly."

South Caroliniana Library

At seventeen, Pamela—though an expert rider—had suffered a spinal injury in a fall from her horse. Her condition gradually worsened, making her a semi-invalid.

When her parents took her to Philadelphia to a noted physician, Pamela began to divide her time between there and South Carolina.

In 1853 when Mrs. Cunningham was making a return trip to Rosemont by steamer, she floated down the Potomac River and passed Mount Vernon, the former home of George Washington. She had visited there in her childhood and more recently had returned with her family. It distressed her to see the historic site in such disrepair. Upon arriving home, she wrote her daughter, "Even in the moonlight I could see the sagging roof and the collapse of one of the stately columns. If the men of this country cannot keep it in repair, why can the women not do it?"

Inspired by her mother's words, Pamela took up the challenge. She now had a purpose for living, and her whole being quickened with the thought.

Upon hearing of her plans, friends concerned for her health tried to dissuade her, but she was not to be stopped.

Writing as "A Southern Matron," Miss Cunningham called on the "Ladies of the South" to raise money to purchase the historic site and restore it. Her letter appeared in the *Charleston Mercury* on December 2, 1853. In that day and time, it was proper for a lady's name to appear in a newspaper but three times: at birth, marriage, and death. Yet, Miss Cunningham's letter was so effective that other papers printed it. Shortly afterward women from the North as well as the South, organized. In 1855 clubs formed in Philadelphia placed boxes in Independence Hall to collect coins for restoring Mount Vernon. School children responded to the request that each child give a dime.

In spite of the interest in the project, reaching the goal grew long and difficult. To begin with, the owner of Mount Vernon did not want to sell the estate to a group of women. Even if they could raise the money to buy it, he said, they would not be able to maintain it permanently. Also, getting a charter from the Virginia Legislature giving ladies the right to hold property was a problem.

Finally, Miss Cunningham persuaded the Reverend Doctor Edgar Everett, an orator and former governor of Massachusetts and United States senator, to speak on their behalf. When an acceptable charter finally came through, Miss Cunningham had Lawyer James L. Petigru of South Carolina draw up a constitution.

In 1858 the Mount Vernon Ladies' Association purchased the estate with its two hundred acres of land for $200,000.

During this time Miss Cunningham had remained in Philadelphia, but with the death of her father she found it necessary to return to South Carolina to assume the responsibility of Rosemont.

The Civil War intervened and plans for Mount Vernon had to wait. It was chiefly through appeals to both the Blue and the Gray that the shrine to the father of the country was not destroyed.

In 1867 Miss Cunningham moved into Mount Vernon to serve as resident director of restoration and refurnishing. After twenty years she resigned as regent and returned to Rosemont to write the history of the Mount Vernon Ladies Association. Unfortunately, she did not have the strength to do it. During this time Miss Cunningham was often ill. She wrote to friends of spending much of her winters with her head encased in scarfs to overcome chills and of having to remain in a dark room for long periods.

Ann Pamela Cunningham died May 1, 1875, and was buried in the First Presbyterian Church yard in Columbia. Her family home burned in 1930. A monument to her, "Ann Pamela Cunningham, the Southern Matron," stands on the site.

A portrait of this persevering lady hangs in the Senate Chamber and in the Governor's Mansion, as well as in Mount Vernon.

South Carolinians visiting George Washington's home in Virginia can be proud that a woman from Laurens County made it all possible.

Mary Boykin Chesnut

KEEPER OF DIARY
1823–1886

Mary Chesnut awoke with a start at the Mills House in Charleston. Lying in bed, she listened intently. Saint Michael's chimes struck four in the morning.

South Caroliniana Library

And then she heard it again—the loud noise that had awakened her. It was the boom of a cannon—there was no doubt about it this time.

Suddenly the inn came alive with hurrying footsteps. "Oh, Lord, protect us," she breathed. Throwing on a doublegown and shawl, she hurried with the others to the rooftop. In the harbor shells burst in an attack on Fort Sumter. The time was April 1861. The Civil War had begun.

Mary was born to an aristocratic, wealthy family on March 31, 1823, in the small community of Statesburg near Camden, South Carolina. From a very early age she was an avid reader.

Shortly before her ninth birthday, she wrote to her father, a United States senator:

> Mother says she received a letter from you this morning and says you have been speaking on the tariff I will read my Fathers speech when it is published.

Mary's writing may have been deficient in punctuation, but the fact that an eight-year-old planned to read her father's speech in the newspaper tells us much about her.

At thirteen Mary attended Madame Talvande's School in Charleston. At the school she learned French and German, which unlocked the door of much foreign literature for her. It was also at this school that she met James Chesnut, Jr., of Mulberry Plantation near Camden. He was the son of a rich planter, and he had recently graduated from Princeton. The two exchanged poems. Three years later they became engaged. In 1840, after Chesnut returned from study abroad, they were married. She was seventeen; he was twenty-five.

The couple went to Mulberry Plantation, the Chesnuts' country home three miles south of Camden, where James practiced law. Since her husband's parents and two unmarried sisters made their home at Mulberry, Mary had little to do. She spent time making clothes for the slave children and playing the guitar and singing ballads learned as a child. Although the practice was illegal, she undertook the task of teaching the slave children to read.

Even though Mary thought that slavery on the plantations was a great evil, she enjoyed the comforts it gave her. Yet she wrote: "Slaves are more of a care than a blessing. The Negroes benefit more than anyone else as my father-in-law supports the old and the young among them."

Later James Chesnut, Jr., became a United States senator, a post he resigned to help lead the fight for secession. In this pursuit he served as an aide to General P.G.T. Beauregard.

Richmond, the new capital of the Confederate States, was always a favorite place for Mary. Even with the hustle and bustle of carriages at Mulberry, life there lacked the stimulation needed for Mary's intellect. "I hate the dullness of the plantation," she once wrote. "I would sleep on boards if I could once more be amidst the stir and excitement of a live world."

As the wife of a high-ranking officer, Mary was able to move in the world she desired. She and her husband became friends with Jefferson and Varina Davis; consequently, she was at the center of the action during most of the Civil War.

A talented observer, Mary took in everything around her and attempted to write it down in the form of fragmentary prose. The result was two unpublished novels: *The Captain and the Colonel* and *Two Years of My Life*. These attempts at writing fiction and her passion for reading helped Mrs. Chesnut develop the writing skills used in her valuable diary keeping. Entries kept from November 1860 through August 1865 are said to be the most famous war diary of a Southern woman. Portions of her diary first appeared in *The Saturday Evening Post* in 1905. Besides recording her account of the war, *A Diary from Dixie* provided a picture of the society in which she traveled. It covered Montgomery, Alabama, and Richmond, Virginia, as well as Camden and Charleston in South Carolina.

Mrs. Chesnut also published sketches about the war in the Charleston *News and Courier*. An unpublished memoir, *Two Years—Or the Way We Lived Then*, tells of episodes from her childhood and school days.

A sparkling conversationalist, Mary Chesnut loved parties, where she enjoyed observing guests. Of General Robert E. Lee she wrote: "He looks so cold and quiet and grand. I wonder if anyone really knows him. He has no patience with any personal complaints or grievances. He is all for the cause."

With her touch of vanity, Mrs. Chesnut also loved the compliments of Southern gentlemen. Still she resented a society dominated by males. "South Carolina, as a rule," she wrote, "does not think it necessary for women to have any existence outside their pantries and nurseries. But for men the pleasures of the world are reserved."

The Chesnuts had no children, but Mary was devoted to her sister's, whom she called her "Sweet Williams." Upon her death in 1886, she was buried in the Chesnut family cemetery, Knight's Hill, Camden.

Martha Schofield

ABOLITIONIST AND EDUCATOR
1839–1916

Carriage wheels on their drive awakened Martha. She slipped from her bed and moved to her upstairs window. The light from her father's lantern shone on a dark-faced person dressed in her mother's bonnet and shawl. Later Martha was to learn the fugitive waited for Martha's father to spirit her away to Canada and freedom and that the woman's children and husband had been sold to different masters.

With parents like Mary Jackson, an eloquent speaker against injustices, and Oliver Schofield, a Quaker abolitionist, it is no wonder Martha inherited strong feelings of social concern. In fact, Martha's ancestors, who settled in America in the eighteenth century, made known their opposition to slavery. It was her paternal grandfather who made Pine Grove Farm a station for the Underground Railroad. Her maternal grandfather turned his attention to the plight of the American Indian and spent two years instructing them in agricultural and mechanical skills.

Martha, called "Mart" by her father, was born February 1, 1839, at Pine Grove Farm in Buck County, Pennsylvania. Along with her older twin sisters, Sarah and Lydia, brother Benjamin, and a younger sister, Eliza, she spent a largely happy childhood at this brown fieldstone farmhouse—churning butter, gathering nuts, riding hogs in the barnyard, and picnicking along the Neshaminy.

The children's schooling took place in an upper room of the Schofield home. Later Martha attended a school established by her uncle, John Jackson. There she distinguished herself in reading.

From an early age Martha's strong curiosity made her an avid listener, especially of discussions of politics among the famous abolitionists who frequented their home. She and her sisters also caught the spirit of idealism and courage at lectures in nearby Philadelphia. Martha recorded in her journal many of these occasions with Lucretia Mott, William Lloyd Garrison, and others.

Upon the death of Oliver Schofield in the winter of 1852, Mary Jackson sold their farm and moved her five children to Byberry, a Quaker community on the outskirts of Philadelphia. Here they found people who held the same

Schofield School

values and worked ceaselessly for reform. Martha continued her education at Newton, the Friends' school in Byberry.

When Martha was seventeen, Mary moved her family to Darby and their new home, Erminridge, only a block from the fine old Quaker Meeting House. The children proudly accepted their mother's recommendation as a Quaker minister. This meant Mary would now speak in meetings other than her own group. And speak Mary did—on the treatment of the American Indian, the poverty-stricken, the handicapped, and slavery. "It is," she said, "the responsibility of women to eradicate injustice."

Finances made it impossible for Martha to continue advanced study. Like her sisters, she felt a responsibility to contribute to her family's resources as soon as possible. With a natural talent for teaching, she began her career in the Bell School on Long Island. During the winter of 1858, at Bell's, she wrote in her journal. She spoke of sleigh rides, masquerades, dances, and trips to the city but very little of teaching. Invariably Martha was the initiator of games and pranks that filled the evenings.

Later Martha taught in the Willets Female Seminary in Harrison, New York, until frequent bouts of illness made it necessary for her to return home. At twenty-two Martha found herself in a society where marriage and motherhood were the normal pattern at her age. Unsuccessful young ladies accepted a secondary place in society: teachers or maiden aunts helping a married sister with a household of her children.

After disappointments in relationships with men, Martha resigned herself to the solitary life of helping others. Like her idols, Dorothea Dix, Clara Barton, and Louisa May Alcott, she volunteered at the hospital during the Civil War.

Martha's growing absorption with the antislavery movement led her to return to teaching at Bethany School in Philadelphia. Supported by the Society of Friends, the school taught blacks who were already living in freedom.

With the emancipation of slaves came the opportunity to teach the millions of blacks now needing an education. In October of 1865 the Freedmen's Bureau, organized to assist freed slaves, sent Martha and three others to Wadmalaw Island off the coast of South Carolina. Receiving the appointment to teach on one of the sea islands was the answer to Martha's dream. Yet when the time came, she waved a tearful good-by from the steamer taking her south. She felt she was going into former enemy territory to minister to a restless, transient people.

Fifteen hundred blacks had followed Sherman's army in their march to the sea and had been left destitute. Martha was to help in the job of feeding, clothing, and educating these persons. She found only one who could read and write.

Friendships and the beauty of the sea islands helped to compensate for the loneliness and privation. Martha threw herself into her work. Even frequent instances of ingratitude and slovenliness did not diminish her faith.

President Andrew Johnson's amnesty proclamation of 1865 restored plantations to former owners and brought with it reduced activities by the Freedmen's Bureau. Thus, Martha was moved about along the South Carolina coast—to Edisto and Johns Island, as well as Shaw School in Charleston.

In 1867 an epidemic sweeping the South affected Martha's lungs, and she was forced to return home. Still, she clung to her belief of equality for all people. When South Carolina ratified its new constitution giving blacks representation in the legislature, she saw no reason why women should not be entitled to the same.

"I would gladly pay," she remarked, "if *they* would let me vote."

Though still not strong, Martha returned to teaching. The Pennsylvania Freedmen's Relief Association assigned her and Mary Taylor, another teacher who shared her commitment, to the little town of Aiken.

Here Martha was resented. Some white people felt the Northern teachers had come to impart dangerous ideas of social equality rather than academic skills and thereby disturb the good feeling between races.

In spite of difficulties in being accepted and her health problems, Martha was able to continue her work and even add a night school in the fifth year. She made many friends in the black community. The minister of the freedmen's Baptist church, the Reverend J. E. Hayne, became a devoted friend. Also, the influx of winter visitors from the North brought callers, many of whom contributed financially to the school.

With Ulysses Grant's inauguration as president, many Northerners felt the government should support freedmen's schools; consequently, private funds for blacks' education diminished. Some Philadelphia Quakers now concentrated on the plight of the Indian. With the end of the Aiken school inevitable, Martha set about to establish her own school.

Using her business acumen, her portion of her grandmother Schofield's estate, and donations from her home area, she succeeded in constructing a school and a house, which she called Oakwald.

Determined to make her school the best, Martha studied other schools for blacks: Hampton Normal and Agricultural Institute in Virginia, Lincoln University in Pennsylvania. She also attended state and national teachers' conventions.

The new South Carolina constitution stating that education be available for all offered financial hope. The school began to receive some funds. The state also appointed trustees and licensed Martha as a teacher. State funds, however, took care of only a small part of expenses and were not always readily available, even for teachers' salaries.

From the outset, Martha's goal was to train teachers, yet few students could remain in school long enough to graduate. Families needed their children's labor or the money they might earn.

Regardless of the length of time Martha had the students, she was concerned for their moral and physical well being, as well as for their studies. Her students knew she believed in them and what they could accomplish.

Martha was also a realist. She knew the white population depended on the blacks for labor and that in preparing her students to fill these needs, she could also prepare them to earn economic independence. Changing the name of her school to Schofield Normal and Industrial School, she established programs in printing, shoe repair, carpentry, chair caning, and blacksmith work, as well as in housekeeping and laundry. Always her motto was "Labor is honorable." Still, she held on to her teaching program, and in 1908 the State Board of Education granted college status to graduates.

Seeing a larger role for herself, Martha joined the Republican Club in Aiken and spoke out against blacks being harassed at the voting polls. She also became a charter member of the South Carolina branch of the Woman Suffrage Association and the Woman's Christian Temperance Union.

Although Martha's life was that of a career woman, she never abandoned her belief that marriage and motherhood were the true destiny of women.

In latter years she made speeches at other schools for blacks: Lucy Laney in Augusta, George Weaver in Leesville, Anna Dickerson in White Pond, and nearby Bettis Academy. Her favorite themes were "Temperance" and "Thorough."

Before Martha's death at seventy-seven in 1916, she had the assurance that the people she had served responded to her with their whole hearts. On the morning of February 1, a friend went to wake her for a planned birthday celebration. She had died in her sleep. Over a thousand persons filed by her casket softly singing "Steal Away to Jesus" before it began its journey to Philadelphia and the Friends' Burying Ground.

The cupola from one of the original buildings of Schofield School now stands on that campus in Aiken—a memorial to its founder.

Floride Clemson Lee

KEEPER OF DIARY
1842–1871

Floride Clemson sat at her desk in Aunt Elizabeth Barton's boarding school in Philadelphia. Her mother's recent letter lay open before her.

"Now that you are fourteen," it read, "I am sure you will be more occupied with being ladylike. Remember to speak French daily, sit still in the classroom, be respectful, and do not hide your noble qualities under bad rubbish."

Floride sighed. Last week it had been: "Aunt Barton tells me you have been sitting and standing crooked, lounging, face picking, and nail biting. All of this causes me much pain. Remember, Daughter, there is no higher pleasure than having a feeling of conquering ourselves."

Oh, well, she supposed it was a mother's duty to try to make her daughter into a lady.

Floride wondered if Aunt Barton had also written to her mother about last week's outburst in class. When Aunt Barton had called Floride in for consultation about shouting several times at the top of her lungs in her teacher's absence, Floride had lost her self-control. "I don't care," she said to Aunt Barton. "There has to be a black sheep in every school, and I'm that here."

The manner in which Aunt Barton had raised her eyebrows still sent a shiver up Floride's spine.

Anyway, she wasn't rereading her letter for all this reprimanding. She wanted to hear again about her father. She found it now.

"Your father loves you," her mother had written. "It is more evident now that you are not at home to irritate him."

"Your father loves you—"

Although Thomas Greene Clemson had never told his daughter that he loved her, Floride felt that he did, and she wanted very much to please him. It was just that he was always so irritable. Despite what her mother said, it was not she who irritated her father but her chronically ill brother Calhoun.

Too, Floride knew that the death of her grandfather, John C. Calhoun, had worried her father tremendously. As secretary of state, Grandfather Calhoun had made Thomas Clemson charge of affairs in Belgium. Now her father felt his father-in-law's death would affect his future, and this had put him under great mental strain.

South Caroliniana Library

Floride's eyes fell upon the worst part of her mother's letter. "You cannot come home for Christmas because there is no one to escort you."

Pshaw! Floride thought. Why couldn't a girl travel alone if a man could? Besides, she missed her dog Leo, whom she had named for a former tutor.

That she had been sent five dollars and a promise of other gifts was little consolation, and before Floride knew it, she was biting her nails again.

Although the restrictions of the school bothered Floride, two years there did much to mature her. She improved in composition and piano, and developed an outstanding singing voice. She even consented to wearing the detested hoops in her skirts. More importantly, there was an increased understanding between mother and daughter, for in one of Floride's letters to her mother she says, "I would not exchange you for any other mother in the world."

At this time Anna Marie Clemson wanted her daughter to come home. Floride knew her mother was eager to introduce her to Washington society.

This period of Floride's life, however, proved to be an unhappy one. Her younger sister Nina had died after only a few days' illness, and for a while Floride's parents were inconsolable. Also, Floride suffered a painful boil at the base of her spine, as well as a cough that lasted until spring.

In 1859 Floride made a long-awaited visit to her birthplace, her Grandmother Calhoun's home, Fort Hill, in Pendleton District, South Carolina.

All of Floride's relatives were impressed with her height and coloring. Mrs. Calhoun proudly showed off her pretty, talented granddaughter, and Floride loved the attention. She rode horseback and attended dances with a caution that to dance more than once with the same young man would cause "talk."

Floride's mother wrote that her father had been appointed head of the Agriculture Department and as a result was much calmer and happier. This office eventually took her father to Europe to purchase seeds and cuttings.

Because Floride's father was on familiar terms with President James Buchanan, Floride often attended parties and receptions at the White House.

In 1861 South Carolina seceded from the Union. It was rumored that all Southern sympathizers would be arrested and have their property taken. Therefore, the Clemsons had to be extremely careful in their travel and correspondence. People could be taken prisoner merely for writing to friends in the South.

In this same year, Floride's brother Calhoun left the agricultural pursuits with his father to join the Confederate Army. He later became a prisoner of war.

In 1862 Floride began keeping a diary. It told of her trip to Niagara Falls, her journey to Beltsville, Maryland, and her life in Pendleton, South Carolina. This diary has served to give details of life during that period of history. For example, in 1865 tallow candles were used for lighting in Pendleton. There was no regular mail and no newspaper. Confederate money held little value. Even everyday shoes cost sixty to one hundred dollars, and butter was seven dollars a pound.

As did all Southerners of this time, the Clemson family lived in fear of Yankee raids. For many nights in succession, Floride and her family did not take off their clothes. They were especially anxious about jewelry and silver, for the looting soldiers were chiefly in search of those items. Some Southerners destroyed their own storehouses of wine so that the soldiers would not get drunk and go on a rampage. Passing troops always took food and the best of the horses. Some of the now-freed Negroes left with the soldiers.

By taking an oath to be loyal to the Union, the Southerners could be spared much humiliation. However, many Southerners felt the oath to be degrading and refused to take it.

To pass the time, Floride began to draw likenesses of her friends from their photographs. Always interested in fashion, she was delighted when her father came South to tell of Northern styles. The women, he said, were now wearing ridiculously large hoops and small bonnets. Their hair was in frizzled curls.

Just after the death of Grandmother Calhoun in October of 1866, Floride tells in her diary of the celebration in which they marched to honor the Confederate dead. A young lady bore a banner for each soldier killed. The march continued through three graveyards where they placed wreaths on each grave. She reported that General Wade Hampton was handsome and soldierly.

One of her last diary entries tells of a visit she paid to Ann Pamela Cunningham, the South Carolinian who preserved George Washington's Mount Vernon home.

In July 1868 Floride had pneumonia. She recovered enough to be married to Gideon Lee of New York, who was nineteen years older than she. They had one child, Floride Isabella.

Floride Elizabeth Clemson Lee died July 23, 1871, at the age of twenty-nine. She was buried in Raymond Hill Cemetery in Carmel, New York.

Upon her father's death, most of his estate was left to found Clemson Agricultural College, now Clemson University.

Elizabeth Allston Pringle

RICE PLANTER AND AUTHOR
1845–1921

Elizabeth Allston Pringle stood on the narrow plank over the deep ditch running around the dark soil of her rice field. In the late afternoon, cranes and bitterns zigzagged in flight against the hazy, mellow light. She welcomed the fresh air from the sea.

Elizabeth watched as the workers came in from the fields. In her usual poised manner, she greeted each one. "How much did you cut today?" she would ask as she held out candy or a biscuit. Thus Elizabeth made every effort to stir pride and enthusiasm in these paid workers.

Like many Southern women just after the Civil War, Elizabeth used her feminine qualities of tact and strict devotion to her daily chores and farm management to get through the trying time of emancipation.

She did not show resentment for the Negroes' shortcomings; rather, she was sympathetic and considerate in helping them build a new life for themselves.

Elizabeth's father, Robert Francis Withers Allston—statesman, scholar, agriculturist—was a kind man who instilled a love of art, music, and beauty in his children. As a child Elizabeth was educated at home by a tutor and later sent to Madame Togno's boarding school in Charleston.

Widowed six years after her marriage to John Julius Pringle, Elizabeth decided to run a rice-planting operation by herself. Consequently, she purchased on credit two plantations that had been in the family: White House on the Pee Dee River from her husband's relatives and Chicora Wood from hers.

Her love of the land and customs of the South caused Elizabeth to struggle against odds to keep alive rice planting, to restore the old plantations, and to continue to teach good conduct and Christian faith to the now-freed Negroes.

South Caroliniana Library

She was glad she had not listened to family members who had tried to discourage her.

Most importantly, Elizabeth recorded the trials of her endeavors. Her accounts, entitled *Woman Rice Planter*, appeared in 1913. It was written under the name of Patience Pennington, for the Negroes called her "Mis' Pashuns." In a later volume, *The Chronicles of Chicora Wood*, she wrote of personal episodes of her early life and those of her family and friends.

Rice planting in the spring always excited Elizabeth. She liked to see the young Negro girls with bare feet and skirts tied up as they danced about "claying" the rice seed. In this manner they thoroughly mixed the seed with clay water and let it soak over night. This ritual kept the seed from floating when the water was turned into the fields, for birds quickly devoured any floating seeds.

In a field plowed by sturdy oxen, workers scattered rice seed. Then they lifted the field gate, or "trunk," to allow tidewater to cover the rice fields. Even the unpleasant smell of the fields at this time did not lessen Elizabeth's love for the land.

Harvest of the rice came in crisp, cool October. The bowed heads of golden rice grains glistened in the sunlight. With small scythes the workers cut the full-ripe grain and carried the immense loads across the plank bridges to lay it on the stubble to dry. The next day they tied them into sheaves with rice straw.

Prayers went up for fair weather until the rice could be loaded onto large flat-bottom boats propelled by poles and steered by one huge oar at the stern.

After being threshed in the mills, the cracked rice and flour were ready for eating. Some of the rice was saved and "whipped out" for seed, as careful planters of the South did not use the broken threshed rice for seed.

A great storm in 1906 destroyed the banks and flood gates of the rice fields. Now many old rice fields lie under dense overgrowth of water grasses and reeds. Some former rice plantations have become game preserves.

TWENTIETH CENTURY

Today people take for granted a woman's right to be educated, to vote, to earn a salary, to witness a legal document, and to own property. But South Carolina's history shows this has not always been the case. In the past, women were widely regarded as mentally and physically inferior. In the mid-nineteenth century American women were their spouse's legal chattels. A wife's earnings and property, and even her children, belonged to her husband. She could not make a contract nor could she vote. At one time the law allowed a man to beat his wife. It even went so far as to prescribe the size of the stick to be used.

Women have, through strivings of their own and sometimes with the help of men, gained equality before the law. More importantly, they have gained the dignity of freedom as individuals.

Some have fought against prejudice toward their race, as well as their sex; others for the right to education for all people. Many have used their God-given talents to the glory of their state and the benefit of their fellow citizens.

Whatever the achievement, all have proven that the women of South Carolina are helping to move their state forward.

Matilda Arabella Evans

DOCTOR
CIRCA 1872–1935

Matilda straightened up from the dusty earth, reached under the burlap bag hanging from a thin shoulder strap, and rubbed her aching back. Wearily she gazed over the long rows of cotton.

The shadows of the scratchy stalks grew longer, but it would be at least an hour before the sun set, sending them in from the fields.

"Matilda," her mother's mellow voice called from across the rows, "you remember, Child, you need to fill your bag again, and we still have hay to mow. Work hard now. I don't want you spending your life in nobody else's cotton patch."

Matilda sighed, shifted the slender strap to a fresh spot across her shoulder, and bent low to pull the fluffy cotton spilling from the bolls. She did so look forward to going back to the Schofield Boarding School. More than anything she wanted to get an education. She knew that her parents, Andrew and Harriet Evans, also held that dream for her. But why did it have to be so hard?

After high school at the Schofield school in Aiken, Matilda left Aiken County for Oberlin College in Ohio. There she worked her way through college by waiting tables. Upon graduation she returned to Schofield to teach. While there,

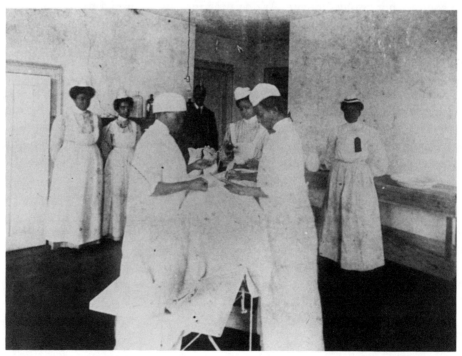

Matilda Evans in the operating room   *Palmetto Leader*

South Caroliniana Library

she wrote *Pioneer Educator*, the story of Martha Schofield, a Pennsylvania Quaker who in 1868 founded the school, one of the first high schools for Negroes.

Schofield Industrial School, as it came to be called, offered carpentry, farming, harness making, blacksmithing, wheelwrighting, shoemaking, sewing, cooking, millinery, housekeeping, and laundry work, as well as credits for teaching.

After another year of teaching in Miss Lucy Laney's School in Augusta, Georgia, Matilda yearned to do something further with her life. Consequently, she enrolled in Women's Medical College in Pennsylvania and received her medical degree in 1897. She was the only Negro in her class. After graduation, Dr. Evans moved to Columbia, where she was the first native black woman doctor in the state. Lucy Hughes Brown was actually the first black doctor to practice in the state, but Matilda was the first South Carolinian to do so.

In her younger days Matilda Evans had wanted to become a medical missionary to Africa. Although she didn't pursue that dream, she became an apostle of sanitation and better living conditions. In 1932 she founded Evans' Clinic at 1235 Harden Street in Columbia. With others she established the Zion Church Clinic, where poor children received treatment. She also founded Taylor Lane Hospital, the first black hospital in Columbia, and the nurses' training school once located at the intersection of Taylor Street and Two-Notch Road.

Her home, "Cottage Inn," served as an open house for youth. She started a place for underprivileged boys to swim, and after teaching herself to swim by reading an article, she taught the boys. She also owned and operated Lindenwood Farm off Two-Notch Road, where she raised chickens, cows, pigeons, vegetables, and fruit trees.

Besides her work as a doctor for more than thirty-seven years, Matilda Evans served as an officer in the Episcopal Church, as president and organizer of the Colored Congaree Medical Society, and as a trustee of Haynes College in Augusta, Georgia. During World War II her volunteer work in the Medical Corps won her a commission.

Dr. Evans also founded a weekly newspaper, *The Negro Health Journal of South Carolina.*

After a life of service to others, Matilda Arabella Evans died on November 17, 1935. She is buried in the Palmetto Cemetery in Columbia.

Mary McLeod Bethune

EDUCATOR
1875–1955

Mary Jane's bare, dusty feet danced along the dirt road winding between the cotton patches near Mayesville, South Carolina. Some yards ahead her mother walked in her regal manner, a load of wash balanced on her head.

Now and then Patsy McLeod lifted a slender arm to steady the freshly done clothes. Turning, she urged her young daughter along.

"What's keeping you, child?" Her mother's voice was gentle. She was a descendant of an African prince and had inherited a royal bearing and a quick intelligence. Mary Jane's father, Samuel, had fallen in love with her mother and had been allowed by his master to buy her from a nearby plantation.

"I'm dreaming—" Mary Jane answered. "Dreaming 'bout God." Her almost purple-black little face beamed under tight black braids.

As they rounded the curve, the Wilsons' big white house came into view. Mary Jane's smile faded. The big house was many, many times larger than the McLeod cabin with its seventeen children.

Mary Jane followed her mother as she stepped off the gravel driveway leading

South Caroliniana Library

up to the white columns and onto the footpath to the rear entrance of the Wilsons' home.

While her mother delivered the wash inside, Mary Jane busied herself trying to dodge away from a blue-bellied fly that circled her head. Then she saw the playhouse of the white children. She went over, and under the gaze of the golden-haired Wilson children, she inched her way in. Her eyes widened at all the toys, especially the dolls with their furniture.

"Would you like to hold one of my dolls?" one asked.

"Yes, Ma'am," Mary Jane said as she settled into a chair that just fit and waited for the doll with its silk and ruffles to be placed in her lap.

It was then she saw the book. Instinctively, she reached out and picked it up. The golden-headed little girl flounced across the room to snatch it from her hand.

"Put that book down!" she cried out. "*You* can't read!"

That night Mary Jane sat on the doorsill in the July dusk hugging her knees and staring at the stars. Her older sisters had just burned smoke sticks–rags soaked in crude oil and wrapped around kindling tips—to keep the mosquitoes away, and the air reeked of the smell.

Of all the McLeod children, Mary Jane was the strangest and the most energetic. She worked harder in the fields; she prayed harder. Her mother once said, "This child has a rising soul. She will either go far or get her heart broken."

The Carolina moon shone down on Mary Jane as she thought of the little Wilson girl's stinging words. "*You* can't read!"

"I will so learn to read," Mary Jane said aloud. "Then I can read our Bible to Grandmother Sophia."

How many hours had she spent by her grandmother, the old woman's wiry gray-wool hair wrapped in a red bandanna and her long-stemmed pipe clutched between toothless gums? How many times had Grandmother Sophia told her about Queen Esther pleading with the king for her people? Then they would end up singing spirituals.

Yes, she would learn to read. Not a grown-up black person in the town of Mayesville could read. There were no schools for blacks, but somehow, some way she would do it. Hadn't she been the first child in her family to be born into freedom?

Fortunately, after the Civil War and the Thirteenth Amendment to the Constitution, which gave slaves their freedom, Mary Jane's father had been allowed by his master to buy land.

Thus, the McLeod children did backbreaking farm labor from sunup to sundown. Mary Jane was a strong, husky girl, who at the age of nine could pick 250 pounds of cotton a day. When their old mule died, she helped to replace it by taking her turn at putting the traces over her shoulders and pulling the plow.

During all this time, Mary Jane never forgot her faith in God or herself. Waiting for her turn to wash her hands in the wooden tub or to be seated at the table to eat hot rice and black-eyed peas (All the children could not eat at one sitting), she hummed her songs and dreamed.

When she was eleven, the Mission Board of the Presbyterian Church opened a school for black children in Mayesville. The teacher, Miss Emma Wilson, combed the countryside looking for students. The McLeod family decided they could spare one, and knowing Mary Jane's desire to learn, allowed her to go.

"Rise and shine and give God the glory!" Mary Jane sang while she plucked the puffy white cotton bolls and stuffed them into the burlap bag hanging over her shoulder.

Because she had to help finish the season's work, school was a few weeks along when Mary Jane took her place on the bench of the two-room school building. She had never heard a black woman called "Miss" before, and this made a powerful impression on her.

School lasted only four months, as the parents needed their children to help with the crops, and Mary Jane never missed a day after she began. No matter how cold it was, she walked five miles each day.

After supper the entire family gathered around so Mary Jane could impart to them what she had learned.

As the seasons passed, she became the center of their little community. Neighbors brought their problems to her to be solved: the weight and price of their cotton, their debts at the village store, their share of crops just cultivated.

After her help, the group often harmonized on "We Are Climbing Jacob's Ladder," with Mary Jane's strong contralto blending in.

By the time she was fourteen, she had taken every subject Miss Wilson offered. For a while it looked as though her schooling would end, but a concerned lady in Denver, Colorado, offered to pay for the education of one Negro girl "who would make good." Miss Wilson chose Mary Jane to go to Scotia Seminary in Concord, North Carolina.

When her day of departure came, her black friends and relatives for miles around gathered at the station to see her off.

At Scotia, Mary Jane stared in amazement. Her room was on the fourth floor of Faith Hall, and she had never climbed a flight of stairs! What's more, there were real beds and mattresses.

Everybody ate together in a large dining hall. The long table had a white cloth and flowers. Each person had a knife, spoon, and fork. Finally, Mary Jane confessed to her teacher that she had never used a fork.

Mary Jane McLeod spent seven years at Scotia. These years brought about many changes in her thinking and her personality. Sometimes she found that learning could be painful. Once she received a demerit for bellowing out at a friend rather than speaking softly.

By the time she returned home to Mayesville, she had been granted a scholarship to Moody Bible Institute and would leave again for Chicago.

News of her return spread like wildfire, and she worked tirelessly holding classes for family and friends.

Although Mary, as she was called now, was the only black student at Moody Bible Institute, she found love for everyone. Many of the classes at this school involved missionary work, and Mary hoped to go to Africa as a missionary when she graduated. To her disappointment, however, there was no opening for a Negro in Africa.

Instead, she took a teaching position at Haines Normal Institute in Atlanta, founded by Lucy Laney.

Later on, while teaching in Sumter, South Carolina, Mary met and married a fellow teacher, Albertus L. Bethune, and they had a son. Still a teacher at heart, Mary dreamed of beginning her own school. When she was asked to move to Florida and run a small parochial school, she accepted.

Finally, in 1904 she found the place she had longed for. With $1.50 and much faith in God, she started Daytona Educational and Industrial Training School for Negro Girls in Daytona, Florida.

With simple supplies such as charred splinters for pencils, ink from elderberries, and desks of discarded packing crates she started the school of her dreams. The girls gathered moss from live oaks to stuff into mattress covers for beds and baked sweet potato pies to sell to the workmen along the railroad tracks to help meet their expenses.

Around the school Mrs. Bethune became known as a "dirt chaser," for she inspected everything and everybody for cleanliness. If she saw a scrap of paper on the campus, she would march toward it and scoop it up. "How could you look at it and not pick it up?" she would demand of anyone near her.

"I am going to teach my girls crafts and homemaking," Mrs. Bethune said. "They will be trained in head, hand, and heart: their heads to think, their hands to work, and their hearts to have faith."

Mrs. Bethune made friends with some of the resort owners in Daytona, and they made contributions to her school. Among her benefactors were James M. Gamble, Thomas H. White, and the Rockefellers. Her benefactors helped organize a biracial board of trustees, and the school grew into an accredited four-year college. In 1923 it merged with Cookman Institute for Boys in Jacksonville to become Methodist-affiliated Bethune-Cookman College.

Within five years Mrs. Bethune had founded five mission schools staffed by her students, had begun a small hospital for blacks, and had become active in many national clubs. Now she urged blacks to vote.

One night before national elections in 1920 the Ku Klux Klan, a group of hooded white men organized to frighten blacks into obedience, appeared at her school. Mrs. Bethune had her staff turn on all the lights in the school and sing a hymn. She herself stood in the light and faced the procession of about eighty shrouded men.

"We're warning you," said a muffled voice from behind a mask. "Stop trying to get 'Niggers' to vote, or we'll burn your buildings right to the ground."

"Burn them if you must, you cowards," she railed. "I'll build them right back. The forces of evil shall not prevail."

The men hesitated and the flicker of torches moved away.

"They've left a can of kerosene," someone said.

"Good," Mrs. Bethune remarked. "We can always use extra fuel."

The next day a long line of blacks waited at the polls to vote.

As the events unfolded to reveal Mrs. Bethune's true greatness, she moved into national affairs. This dynamic personality, characterized by her pompadour hairstyle and a walking cane, became a member of the Executive Board of the National Urban League and the National Association for the Advancement of Colored People. She received the Spingarn Medal Award, presented each year by the NAACP for the highest achievement by an American Negro.

When President Franklin D. Roosevelt established an advisory committee of the National Youth Administration, he named Mrs. Bethune director of affairs. Under her guidance the agency provided educational training for more than six hundred thousand black children each year.

Mrs. Bethune also formed the National Council of Negro Women and helped to draw up the charter for the United Nations. She was one of the founders of the Southern Conference on Human Welfare. She became a frequent visitor to the White House, and a deep friendship formed between her and Mrs. Roosevelt. The President's regard for her is shown in his comment: "I am always glad to see you because you never ask for anything for yourself."

Alt-Lee Studio

Mary McLeod Bethune portrait that hangs
in the S.C. statehouse

Upon the president's death, Mrs. Roosevelt gave Mrs. Bethune his walking cane.

Along with many honorary degrees from colleges, she received the Francis A. Drexel Award in 1936 for distinguished service to her race. Her portrait hangs in the South Carolina State House. Washington, D.C., has a monument showing her hand outstretched to some black children.

No matter how many other responsibilities Mrs. Bethune assumed, her students came first. She knew the young people she was training would go out and carry on her life's work.

In 1950 when she returned to Mayesville for a visit, she was as much at home in the sharecropper's cabin as she was in the White House, for she never grew away from her people. One of the most treasured among her eight honorary doctorates was from South Carolina State College in 1930.

On May 18, 1955, Mrs. Bethune was rocking on the porch of her home at Bethune-Cookman College in Daytona Beach when she suffered a fatal heart attack. She is buried on the grounds of the school she founded.

How far this little girl in her feed-sack dress had come—*and had brought her people*—from the playhouse episode of "*You* can't read!"

In March of 1985 a stamp commemorating Mary McLeod Bethune was issued by the United States Postal Service, and postal officials held a ceremony honoring her in Mayesville, the Sumter County town where she was born.

Alice Ravenel Huger Smith

WATERCOLORIST
1876–1958

Alice straightened up from her "wrapping paper" easel, rubbed her neck in weariness, and leaned once again over the sketch of the Charleston "Flower Woman." Now she knew why her parents had been startled by her announcement that she wanted to open an art studio. They had not wanted to see her struggle to become a self-supporting artist.

Still, sheer determination drove her like an obsession. Day after day she designed dance programs, tally cards, fan and glove cases, and painted the black "flower women" on the streets of Charleston. The portraits of the women were quick sales at a dollar each; thus, she drove herself to paint as many as she possibly could each week. The work paid for her small room in the Confederate Home and College and for her saucers of paint. In spite of her long hours and hard work, the purse was lean.

Yet Alice's current work was not her goal. She longed to paint landscapes of her beloved Lowlands. Her schooling at the Carolina Art Association, accepted training for well-bred young ladies of her time, had given her not only the fundamentals of art, but it had succeeded in fanning the smoldering fire of her dream. Being brought up surrounded by the beauty of the wind-tossed palmettos, the mighty surge of the ocean's waves, and the pervading ricefields made an indelible impression on Alice. That, along with her love of reading and the charm of their spacious home, developed in her a sense of the poetry of life.

Lack of formal training did not deter Alice in her goal to capture on her easel the land she loved. Excited by her "calling," she stole at sunrise to watch herons in the black waters of a cypress swamp or to gaze upon a lake of floating pink lotus. She sat in the woods with notebook and pencil to record the pose of a cardinal or an oriole. She went on country expeditions to impress atmosphere, light, and mood on her memory. Visits to humble homes of black families, buggy rides, boat trips into the marshes, moonlight walks on the beaches—all of these Alice observed, and she made notations, particularly of the colors of nature, in her sketch book.

Upon returning to her studio, the artist transferred her impressions to the ethereal water colors in which her talent reached its peak.

Other days she visited relatives' plantations where she combed the countryside, observing blacks at work and studying rice fields.

During this time, orders for copying ancestors' portraits poured in, and in accepting them Alice developed a technique for reproducing in water color the quality of old, time-mellowed oil paintings.

Always the serious artist, Alice was critical of her own work and eager to

learn more. When a visitor from the North lifted eyebrows at her little japanned box holding her paints, she hurried to King Street and bought a meat platter, tubes of paints, and larger brushes.

Hearing of the arrival in Charleston of a renowned painter, a Mr. Harrison from Woodstock, New York, Alice went to his villa to ask for lessons.

"No," he told her, "I have run away for a rest. But I will talk with you now and then about what you are trying to do. I'll even quarrel with you a bit."

In one of their dialogues, he announced: "Moss is not paintable."

"But that is just how I feel about snow," Alice replied.

Under his influence Alice did fewer, smaller sketches and thought more of the placing of colors. "My work is like cobwebs," she wrote of her gray, fragile painting with threadlike leaves and branches of Spanish moss on the trees of Wappaoolah, a relative's plantation.

The feeling of solitude in her water colors gave Alice's paintings the effect of Japanese landscapes. Thus, it seemed inevitable that the artist would study Japanese art, including woodcuts. With Motte Alston Read, a scientist with the temperament of an artist, she gained knowledge and mastery of Japanese line and color, which became of highest worth to her in her own paintings. Her own woodblock prints gained the attention of museums and collectors.

Under the influence of Helen Hyde and Bertha E. Jaques, both etchers, Alice became the first Charlestonian to learn the technique of etching.

Always generous with her time, Alice shared her knowledge with aspiring painters and fellow artists. At this time she shared a studio on Atlantic Street with Anna Heyward Taylor, Leila Waring, and Elizabeth O'Neill Verner, a former student of hers. Their "studio teas" encouraged an interest in the arts.

Still, Alice's dream was to paint landscapes. In 1913 she fulfilled this dream by illustrating Elizabeth Allston Pringle's *A Woman Rice Planter* with sketches of the rice country and its inhabitants. She also illustrated *The Carolina Low Country,* by Augustine T. Smythe, and *Adventures in Green Places* and *A Carolina Rice Plantation of the Fifties,* by Herbert Ravenel Sass.

Working with her father, Daniel Elliott Huger Smith, in 1917, she illustrated and published jointly *Twenty Drawings of the Pringle House, Dwelling Houses of Charleston,* and the historical volume *Charles Fraser.*

From the 1920s on, recognition came to "Miss Alice." Fellow artists and admirers came to know the warm understanding, keen intellect, and fun-filled humor in this delicate-framed artist.

The years that followed brought the loss of eight family members and proved to be a noncreative time. But when Alice did take up her brush again, dinner plates rather than saucers held her palette. Her pictures went on tour, first to Southern cities, then to capitals in the North, West, and finally abroad. She became a popular speaker at clubs and in colleges. Mount Holyoke in Massachusetts honored her with a doctorate of letters.

A civic-minded person, Miss Alice held memberships in the historical society, the museum, and the poetry society. She was an incorporator of the Historic Charleston Foundation and an organizer of exhibitions for the Carolina Art Association. The Charleston Federation of Women's Clubs inducted her into their hall of fame.

The war years of the early forties found Miss Alice and her sister Caroline—an

accomplished musician—offering a "touch of home to soldiers away from home" at historic 69 Church Street. A familiar sight was Miss Alice sitting on her joggling board in her back garden telling tales of the Low Country to soldiers faced with the turbulent times of World War II. A scrapbook of letters from these far-flung friendships express appreciation for the sisters' Southern hospitality at a most-needed time.

In 1950 Alice compiled and edited her father's memoirs. On her birthday in 1956, friends wrote their love and admiration into a biography of her. "Throughout my life," Miss Alice said, "I have been trying to paint the rice planting section of South Carolina, that long, flat strip of lowlands lying within the influence of the tides."

This author, illustrator, printmaker, and painter achieved her goal. For in painting what she knew about and loved, she captured "fleeting" images for posterity. A flock of wild turkeys disappearing in a neglected field of broom grass, the Low Country's winter dawn, the opalescent mist brooding over marshes, golden rice fields, and the lonely reaches of the sea—all took on a magic under her brush.

Before her death in 1958, Miss Alice gave many family heirlooms to the Charleston Museum. She also contributed a set of water colors, done to illustrate the Sass' book, to the Carolina Art Association. Portfolios of these paintings are now sold through the Gibbes Art Gallery in Charleston.

Anna Hyatt Huntington

SCULPTOR
1876–1973

Ann Vaughn Hyatt Huntington was born in Cambridge, Massachusetts, on March 10, 1876. As soon as she could crawl, she inspected horses' hoofs; before she could swim, she peered so intently at a swarm of minnows that she toppled off the family dock into the running tide.

At an early age Anna learned the power of observation from her paleontologist father, Alpheus Hyatt. As a lover of animals, Anna had a kind of silent communication with them.

Her love of art came from her painter mother, Audella Beebe Hyatt. Accepting the nickname of "Clam," due to her shyness, she let the animals she sculpted speak for her.

When Anna's sister Harriet, who was eight years older, introduced her to sculpture, Anna gave up her study of violin for working with clay. Yet she felt her musical training gave rhythm to her art. Both sisters studied under Henry Hudson Kitson, the sculptor of the Minute Man statue at Lexington. While Harriet was interested in figure studies of people, Anna concentrated on animals.

Always ideas whirled in Anna's head. As she did errands, she molded her subjects in her mind's eye. In the evenings when her mother read aloud to the family, she heated a spatula over a blue alcohol flame and molded little animals in wax for casting in bronze at a later time.

In these early days in Massachusetts, Anna's subjects were usually domestic animals about the home, although she did some studies of wild animals as they trained nearby for Bostick's animal show. On her brother's farm in Maryland she became so familiar with the anatomy of horses that she could work from memory.

With her earlier education completed, Anna left for New York. There she shared a third floor studio apartment with three other girls. Each contributed

Brookgreen Bulletin, Marion Boyd Allen

fifty dollars toward the rent. In New York she attended classes at the Art Students' League, where Hermon MacNeil was teaching. At first, sales for her sculptures came slowly. "It was real hard work," Anna said of her earlier years, "but then I'd been very much indulged up until that time."

Subway trips to the Bronx Zoo to study wild animals filled many of Anna's days. She particularly liked the big jaguars.

Anna enjoyed showing her subjects in a variety of ways—sometimes at rest; other times, in motion. The antics of her monkeys and the peculiarities of her goats, kangaroos, and other animals reveal her lively sense of humor.

A piece that always reminded Miss Hyatt of her New York days is the small statue she called "Flapper." A deviation from her animal sculptures, the idea came from a bank advertisement in the newspaper. Action oriented, like most of her works, this one shows a girl with her miniskirt flapping above shapely knees. The flapper struggles to hang on to her umbrella, which is being whipped by a New York wind.

Anna's first major success came when she created the equestrian statue of Joan of Arc. Joan, mounted on a striding horse with his head held high, is rising in her stirrups, sword aloft. Although the judges could hardly believe a woman had actually done the work, it received honorable mention at the Paris Salon of 1910. The honor made an immediate impression, and Anna was chosen as the sculptor of a monument of Joan to be erected in New York at Riverside Drive. For this work the French Government awarded her the decoration of the "Palmes Académiques." A high rank among American sculptors was assured.

Always regarded as an "Animalier," Anna loved to tell—interspersed with her high-pitched laughter—of the time she acquired her own horses for models. She fed them so well they soon grew too sleek and fat for her use.

Anna loved horses. Her life-size fighting stallions stand at the entrance to her beloved Brookgreen.

"If I can put a famous person on a horse, I do," she said.

"Andrew Jackson, Boy of Waxhaws," in the Andrew Jackson State Park near Lancaster, shows Jackson sitting bareback on his horse and looking toward his native hills.

She also did Abe Lincoln on a horse in her sculpture "The Prairie Years," now in Salem, Illinois.

At her family's summer home near Gloucester, Anna began to be more concerned with human forms, often introducing an animal or a bird into the composition. Among these pieces is her "Diana of the Chase," which graces the center of a pool at Brookgreen Gardens.

In 1923 Anna Hyatt married Archer Milton Huntington. Although Anna was listed as one of twelve women who earned more than $50,000 in 1912 and Archer was heir to the fortune of railroad builder Collis Potter Huntington, neither cared for the social activities of the wealthy.

In 1929 as the couple searched for a winter home in a mild climate, they stopped in South Carolina where they saw Brookgreen Plantation, land originally granted to eighteenth-century colonists. The long avenue of huge, moss-laden oaks, the remnants of a formal garden, the abandoned rice fields stretching west—all captured their hearts. They purchased this plantation and three other adjoining ones: The Oaks, Springfield, and Laurel Hill.

At Brookgreen, the early home of the Allstons, Anna designed a garden in the shape of a butterfly. When Mrs. Huntington realized what a perfect setting the gardens offered for sculpture, she decided to share the garden and outdoor museum with other American sculptors.

Mrs. Huntington's work is shown in more than two hundred museums in this and other countries. Many smaller pieces are the proud possessions of schools and colleges. Tamassee DAR School has three statuettes of the artist's grandmothers; the University of South Carolina received "Fillies Playing" and "The Torchbearer," a large bronze; Winthrop has "Toilette Matinals," modeled from the ringtail monkeys the sculptor kept at Atalaya, the Huntingtons' home on the seaside of Brookgreen. She dedicated her "Black Panther" to the 353 Fighter Squadron at Myrtle Beach Air Force Base.

The Huntington estate in Redding, Connecticut, also displays her statues.

Her many honors include a gold medal from the American Academy of Arts and Letters, a medal of honor from the National Sculpture Society, and the Grand Cross of King Alfonso of Spain. The universities of Syracuse and South Carolina awarded her honorary degrees, and South Carolina named its music and art gallery for her. She was also inducted into the South Carolina Hall of Fame.

Anna Vaughn Hyatt Huntington, this woman of fragile stature and soft, gentle nature, died on October 4, 1973. She is buried in Woodland Cemetery in New York. Open to the public, Brookgreen Gardens is located eighteen miles south of Myrtle Beach at Murrells Inlet.

Julia Mood Peterkin

AUTHOR
1880–1961

The sun glistened on Julia Mood Peterkin's red hair as she moved erectly along on a visit to the row of servants' houses on Lang Syne Plantation. Because of the frequent illness of her husband, Julia had to be in charge of the 450 blacks, many descendants of former slaves.

In 1903, when tall, lithe Julia married William George Peterkin, a planter and owner of Lang Syne, her life had been quite different. Julia was born in Laurens County on October 31, 1880, to Dr. Julius Andrew and Alma Archer Mood. Sadly, her mother died giving her birth. A remarkable old black "mauma," as such nurses were known, cared for Julia and her older sister. From this wise woman Julia acquired a wealth of folklore: customs, superstitions, and attitudes. When alone with her nurse, Julia spoke Gullah.

While growing up, she was not particularly interested in books. She worked hard in her studies because her older sister did, and Julia admired her. After graduating from Converse College at sixteen, she went on to earn a master's degree. Being interested in drama, she acted in Town Theater productions in Columbia. A year later she taught in a one-room school in Fort Motte.

When Julia was first married and even when she began to look after the needs of the workers on their plantation, she had no intention of writing. In fact, she felt burdened by her task. But the more she visited them, caring for

South Caroliniana Library

the sick, sharing their joys and sorrows, and being lawyer, counselor, friend, and doctor to them, the more she learned to really *see* and *hear* them.

In fact, Julia's literary career appears to have come about from a series of misfortunes: her husband's lengthy illness, the loss of their plantation foreman, and an epidemic among farm animals. All of these circumstances combined threw her into a period of self-examination. As a result, Julia decided to resume her study of music, pursued in earlier years but dropped. Dr. Henry Bellaman, her music teacher and a writer of fiction, urged Julia to write down some of the incidents she would tell him about the workers on the plantation.

The more she thought of his suggestion, the more intrigued she became. All the books she had read depicted Negroes as lazy and sleepy with a tendency to steal and a love for singing and dancing. They were never presented as individuals. Consequently, Julia began to record, in their own speech, what some of the black people thought and said. Her first writing was free verse based on the sayings of her cook. With this new interest, she joined the Poetry Society.

Carl Sandburg's appreciation of her Gullah stories and sketches led to their publication in the magazine *Smart Set* and *The Reviewer*.

Maum Lavinia Berry, the nurse for Julia's only son William, Jr., became the model in her works of fiction. In 1924 she published a collection of short stories, entitled *Green Thursday. Black April* followed in 1927.

Also in 1927 Converse College awarded Mrs. Peterkin an honorary degree. During the summer of that year she accepted an invitation to write at the MacDowell Colony in New Hampshire. There she worked on her book *Scarlet Sister Mary* and enjoyed the friendship of DuBose Heyward, Charlestonian and author of *Porgy*. In 1929 Julia won a Pulitzer Prize for this novel. The honor made her a national celebrity. This third book also became a New York play.

Other works included *Bright Skin* in 1932 and *Roll, Jordan, Roll*, a book of nonfiction in 1933.

All Julia Peterkin's writings prove her to be a pioneer in her interpretation of the South Carolina Negro. Her books were the first from any region to consider the mind and the soul of the plantation black. Frank Durham, who edited a collection of her short stories, said of her: "She saw the Negro as a human being at a time when in the South it was neither the social nor the literary fashion to do so." She showed her Gullah blacks as they were born, worked, loved, suffered, and hoped.

Julia's viewpoints caused much controversy. Some people denounced her because they felt no Southern lady should know so much about the things Julia Peterkin wrote about. Some Southern libraries barred her books, and the local press avoided mentioning them. Julia's comment was, "I mean to present these people in a patient struggle with fate, not in any race conflict."

In fact, Julia came to know blacks so well that one of them remarked, "Miss has got a white skin for-true, but I believe her heart is as black as my own." Others said she was born with a caul on Halloween.

Finally, in recognition of her literary fame, she received praise as the "Pride of South Carolina," and more recently as a literary craftsman.

Besides writing, Julia Mood Peterkin grew roses and raised Llewellyn setters, pigeons, and white Holland turkeys. She also did beautiful embroidery.

With silver streaking her hair, Julia was still regal when she died on August 10, 1961, shortly before her eightieth birthday. She is buried at Fort Motte.

Jane Harris Hunter

SOCIAL WORKER
1882–1971

Nine-year-old Jane Harris clamped her hands over her ears and tried to concentrate on the four o'clock bush outside their meager home. She hated it when her father went on one of his rampages. With his last blow of the ax he had destroyed her sewing machine, his gift after the sale of his last crops.

In spite of her father's violent temper, Jane loved Edward Harris with all her heart. As the son of an English plantation overseer and a Negro slave, Harris was light-complexioned. Everybody said Jane, whom he lovingly called "Sing," was his "spit and image."

In Jane's early childhood, her father farmed as a sharecropper on the Woodburn Farm near Pendleton, South Carolina. A hard-working man, he sacrificed to give his children, Winston, Jane, Rosa, and Rebecca, every advantage. When her parents were not quarreling over her mother's behavior at one of the "hot suppers" or the attention another man had paid her, the household was happy and united. In winter they sat around the fire telling riddles and singing; in summer the children hunted frogs along the meadow streams.

It did seem to Jane, however, that her mother punished her far more than she did the other children, and she lived in fear of these punishments. It was not until many years later that Jane decided it was perhaps her resemblance to her father and their close relationship that caused her mother to feel that the two of them sided against her. Whatever the reason, the strife cast a shadow over Jane's childhood.

In spite of her sometimes childlike emotions, Harriet Milliner kept their two-room dwelling scrupulously clean. She saw to it, too, that the children kept the floors of their cabin scrubbed and the yard swept with homemade brooms.

Not far from the Harris' home on the sloping field, a clay road led to her grandparents' log cabin, the first in the region to be owned by former slaves. Grandmother Milliner was part Cherokee Indian. A midwife, she herself bore nineteen children. Great-grandma Cumber, one hundred and eleven years old, lived with Jane's family, and Jane remembered how she always sent her to bring water from the spring. Jane was deathly afraid of snakes lurking there, but remembering the switch tied to Grandma Cumber's waist, she always obeyed. Her reward was fresh buttermilk and a hunk of corn pone baked in ashes.

In 1889 when Jane was seven, her father sold their farm and moved the family into Pendleton so his children could attend school at Silver Springs Baptist Church. He got a job digging ditches, and Jane's mother became a cook.

The children's schooling, however, was short-lived. Jane's father became angry with his wife's employer when she wanted to take Jane to live in their home. Consequently, he quit his job and moved his family back to a farm near their old place.

Although times were hard, Jane remembers singing with the rich voices of the other cotton pickers. Often she would get so caught up in "Oh, Lawd, Won't You Hear Me Pray" and her favorite, "Walk Together, Children, Don't Get Weary," that she would forget to pick cotton.

Before long, the family moved again, and Jane's father found a job as a hod-carrier with a firm building Clemson College. Her mother took in washing,

Augusta Chronicle

which she did at a nearby spring.

In clothes made from worn sheets and jeans, the children entered school. Jane remembers her brother as a good speller, but she often missed—receiving a whack for every wrong letter. Nevertheless, she was happy to be going to school.

The school times were once more cut short in 1892 when Edward Harris died of jaundice.

Harriet Harris gave up their home, farmed the children out with relatives, and went to Clemson to cook for the Calhoun family.

From her aunt's home Jane was sent to keep house for a Wilson family for room and board. She felt her childhood was over. At ten she cooked, cleaned, washed, and ironed for a family of six and looked after two young children. Her only happy memory of the time was of the oldest Wilson girl teaching her how to read nursery rhymes.

When her mother, who had now remarried, became ill, Jane returned to Clemson to care for her.

A year later at the invitation of another aunt, she went to Charleston, where she watched after a little girl of a well-to-do black family. For Jane it was months of humiliation as she felt the sharp contrast of the child's silk and satin and her own bare feet and ragged clothing.

For a while afterward Jane worked as a chambermaid in a hotel until still another aunt who lived near Woodburn Farm came for her.

At Aunt Caroline's on the Smythe Plantation she helped do laundry for other families and made butter by skimming the cream from the top of milk. She also worked in the field with Uncle Abe, cutting corn for the silo, hoeing, picking cotton, and the worst job, stripping fodder. The sharp blades stung her neck and hands.

A young man who married into the family was writing Negro spirituals. He invited Jane and other young people to sing for him. For that he paid Jane twenty-five cents, as much as she could earn cutting a load of wood.

While at Aunt Caroline's, Jane joined King's Chapel of the African Methodist denomination, yet she felt she lacked personal convictions.

When Jane was fourteen years old, two Presbyterian missionaries, the Reverend and Mrs. E.W. Williams, visited in her relatives' home. Impressed with Jane's desire to please, they proposed a plan for her to attend their boarding school in Abbeville. With only a few months at Silver Spring School and three years at Pendleton County School, Jane was eager to go. Aunt Caroline prevailed upon Jane's mother for permission, and by working at the Smythe Plantation for two dollars a month, Jane was able to save money for clothes and railroad fare.

In the fall of 1896 she entered Ferguson and Williams College, where she was assigned to the senior class in the high school connected with the college. English was difficult for her, but she excelled in arithmetic and history. She most enjoyed public speaking and music. To chant the old spirituals took her back to the happy days of her childhood.

For her board and tuition at the college Jane worked in the dining room and did washing and ironing for the Williams family.

Having inherited something of her father's temperament, Jane remembers writing "I am as stubborn as a mule" over and over for a teacher.

On a more pleasant note, she was selected to recite Tennyson's "The May Queen" and to be crowned during the festivities. Her worries over what she would wear dissolved when a barrel of clothes from the North held the perfect white organdy dress.

When her schooling was over, Jane felt like a motherless child. At Aunt Caroline's home, now filled with other homeless children, she found only a pallet for herself. She wandered to the streams and trees of Woodburn Farm, where she watched cartwhips and snake doctors with their iridescent wings skim over the surface of the water. Under branches of the maples, oaks, and poplars, she remembered learning from her father the healing strength that comes from growing things and the quiet of the woods. She longed for a home to return to.

In August an uncle took her to Florida to help him in his boarding house. After unpleasant experiences with the boarders, she pled with him to send her back to South Carolina, and he did.

In Clemson her mother prevailed upon her to marry Edward Hunter, a kind and fatherly man but forty years older than Jane. For economic reasons she consented.

After a brief unhappy time, Jane left for Charleston to work. There she was a nursemaid to the children of Major and Mrs. Benjamin Rutledge in a lovely home overlooking the Atlantic Ocean. Jane and this family were fond of each other, and Jane helped to send her sisters and brother to her alma mater with the money she earned.

At the suggestion of a friend, Mrs. Ella Hunt, Jane entered the Cannon Street Hospital and Training School for Nurses. Without her vitality and determination, the strenuous labor could have been discouraging. Besides her heavy studies, she cooked, cleaned, and shaved and cut the hair of men patients. When she was singled out by a white surgeon to be his assistant, she worked harder than ever.

Feeling the need for further training, Jane continued her studies at Dixie Hospital and Training School at Hampton Institute in Virginia. The singing of spirituals in the chapel there revived her happier memories of childhood.

Young men from Hampton Institute showed an interest in pretty Jane; but remembering her marriage failure, she did not encourage them.

When her schooling in Virginia was over, Jane again felt she had no place to go. On visiting friends in Richmond, she responded to their request to go with them to Cleveland, Ohio.

There Jane learned firsthand the hardships of the single Negro woman in a large city. She received no encouragement in her applications for a position. Too poor even to afford change for bus fare, she finally took a cleaning job. In Cleveland she joined the Saint John's A.M.E. Church and, through contacts there, obtained a nursing job for a wealthy man. From that she secured other nursing positions. Always on the alert to do her best, she received the unfailing support of physicians. The honor she cherished most was being called upon to nurse Dr. Harlan Pomeroy in his last illness, for his sympathy and friendship had helped to bring her up from poverty to a place of useful service.

Years had softened Jane's resentment toward her mother for her childlike vindictiveness, her opposition to Jane's hunger for knowledge, and her coercing Jane into the loveless marriage. She had come to see that her mother's faults as well as her virtues were the product of her background—a life of hard work rewarded by dancing at "hot suppers."

In 1909 Jane returned to South Carolina and took her mother to Charleston for a visit. However, Harriet Harris was unhappy. Back at Clemson Jane bought land to build her mother a small home to live out her years, but Harriet soon died.

For a time grief and guilt robbed Jane of all interest in her profession. How, she wondered, could she give to the world what she had failed to give her mother? If only she could take up the discords of her life and make harmony out of them.

Finally, she knew what would become her life's work and her salvation; she would start a place of refuge for young Negro girls. How often had she heard of girls being pushed from the nest by economic pressure: alone and friendless in a big city—reduced to squalor and starvation, helpless against temptation and degradation.

With friends in Cleveland Jane formed the Working Girls' Home Association, to provide a place where young unemployed women might find shelter. They would also be taught housekeeping, hygiene, and personal neatness and be given religious training.

Jane suggested the association dues be a nickel because, she said, the project should be the poor helping the poor. The old words and stirring rhythm of "Walk Together Children," which Jane had sung in the cotton field, quickened her spirits and gave her energy to press on.

Ministers in the community consented to be on the advisory board, and Sarah C. Hills, the first white member, gave her support.

In 1919 Jane and the group secured a twenty-three-room house on East Fortieth Street in Cleveland, and the home for girls came into being. They named the association Phillis Wheatley in honor of a slave girl who became America's first important black American poet after being bought and educated by the Wheatley family.

Gradually the association expanded into other buildings. Each time the women rolled up their sleeves to scrape layers of wallpaper and scrub floors.

By 1922 programs of music, handicrafts, and dancing were added and a gymnasium secured. The association opened its doors to church neighborhood clubs, and the Phillis Wheatley Association became a community center. Gifts came from people as diverse as cooks at the home and John D. Rockefeller, Jr. By 1927 the group had built a new home at Cedar Avenue and Forty-Sixth Street.

Jane Hunter's dream had been realized: she had created a haven for homeless girls and offered them opportunities to see the ability and beauty within themselves unfold to make life more beautiful for others.

With activities of the association on an even keel, Jane took courses for self-improvement. In 1925 she graduated from Baldwin-Wallace Law School.

Two schools of higher education awarded her degrees: Wilberforce University and Tuskegee Institute. She participated in many conferences and spoke out for better education. She served as chairman of the committee to study the needs of a Cleveland high school. She also worked to improve the conditions of delinquent Negro girls in the Ohio State School. In her work Jane established inter-racial cooperation and Christian comradeship.

Following Jane Hunter's lead, the National Association of Colored Women established similar homes in nine other cities and made Jane chairman of the Phillis Wheatley Department.

Through it all Jane never forgot her people. She could still picture the cotton pickers stretched across the fields, their heads bent low and sometimes crawling on their knees, but still singing.

All she had accomplished, Jane felt, served as a memorial to the mother she had come to understand late in life. Her autobiography, *A Nickel and a Prayer*, published in 1940, tells the story of her struggle.

Marie Cromer Seigler

GIRLS' CLUB PIONEER
1882–1964

Dear Little Tomato Girl,

Practically all tomatoes have been canned, made into catsup, pickles or preserves. It is now time to complete your work. Make sure you count the visits I made to you.

Be sure your garden measurements are correct. They should be 4,356 feet or 66 feet square.

In trying for the $5.00 prize for the best "Tomato book," use good grade drawing paper about 9" x 11". Make an attractive cover, not too gaudy in color. Use water-color prints and draw in tomatoes. Bind the book at the top with red or green satin baby ribbon or cord.

Of course you will discuss the life and history of tomatoes and of the Aiken County Girls' Tomato Club, the object of the club, and why you enrolled.

The remainder of your book will have facts that will help a tomato grower.

Your book will be judged on neatness, usefulness, beauty, and handwriting.

Don't forget to label all cans before bringing them to the fair.

Aiken county is a great county and you are going to make it greater.

Marie Cromer

With such individual attention, Marie Cromer encouraged her "girls" in the first club of its kind. Known as the Tomato Club and later as the Canning Club, the organized group was a forerunner of the current 4-H Club.

From an early age, when her father's endearing term "Beautiful" was shortened to "Beaut," Marie Cromer possessed a restless desire to *do something* to uplift her generation. This ambition did not lessen during her schooling in

Smithville Township or Abbeville High School, where she was graduated in 1898, or during further education at a small college in North Carolina. Thus, her frequent letters of instruction to her "Tomato Girls" were part of her drive toward culmination of her dream.

One of nine children, Marie Samuella was born on November 9, 1882, to William Oscar and Ella Cox Cromer. She began life on a farm in the Clover Hill Plantation of Abbeville, South Carolina—a land that had nurtured four generations of her family.

In 1907 petite Marie left for Aiken County to teach in a one-teacher school. There she boarded in the Seigler home in Eureka, where young Cecil Hodges Seigler, the superintendent of education of Aiken County, still made his home with his parents.

Here the childhood dream to *do something* erupted into a gnawing desire to broaden visions and remove limitations of the country girls about her. As Marie often said, "I was born in the country. I live in the country, and I know something of its lonesomeness and sleepy-spiritedness. It is because I love the country and its people that I want to do something for the young girls—to help them keep the thinking up when school is over."

At a state teachers' meeting in January of 1910, Marie listened to a speaker tell about the work being done by the Boys' Corn Clubs of America. After hearing wonderful stories of the influence of the boys' clubs—how they had revolutionized agriculture and probably changed the course of many lives— Marie leaped to her feet.

"If the club for boys holds such worth," she questioned, "why not organize a club for girls?"

"I've been asked that question at least fifteen hundred times," the speaker responded. "That's a problem you teachers will have to solve."

"Well," said Marie, "if that's what you're waiting for, I'll certainly do it."

Picking up the challenge, Marie began a one-woman campaign to organize a tomato club for girls. In the evenings and on Saturdays she solicited members until she had enrolled forty-seven. Katie Owens, later Mrs. J.E. Hankinson, was the first member to sign up. One enticement for enrollment was a year's scholarship to Winthrop College for the girl with the best record in cultivation and preservation of tomatoes.

At the time, however, Marie earned only $40 a month. The scholarship would be $140.

While Marie worried about the scholarship funds, each member cultivated her tomato crop on her allotment of one-tenth acre. The only assistance permitted was preparation or plowing of the soil. Each girl must also make a book recording everything from planting the seed through the use of the tomato.

Diligent work from the "Tomato Girls" brought about an abundant yield and with it the need for preserving tomatoes.

In July the Washington office of the Department of Agriculture sent a

Family Photo

canning outfit "as large as a two-horse wagon" to Aiken. The girls' canning club demonstration took place in front of the courthouse in 1910. Eager parents watched and idle onlookers wondered what crazy idea the government was up to now. The bee lasted three days before the equipment was moved to Windsor, where the paring, scalding, filling of cans, tipping and soldering, and setting of cans in boiling water and taking them out continued.

Even without the canning outfit, the girls continued to bring their tomatoes and can all morning. One of the girls acted as hostess for the day. Afternoon picnics gave the canning parties the enthusiasm of a political rally. Sometimes entire communities attended.

This same summer the General Education Board of New York invited Marie to come to their city and others in the Northeast to observe the latest techniques in canning in tin and to learn what other schools were doing in domestic science.

When a county fair served as a showplace for the Boys' Corn Club and the Girls' Tomato Club, the exhibits attracted much attention. Each can or jar of tomatoes held the label "Put up by the Girls' Tomato Club of Aiken County," as well as the girl's autograph.

At the completion of the harvest, fourteen-year-old Katie Gunter of Samaria community near Wagener won the scholarship to Winthrop. Driving a buggy, she brought basket after basket of ripe tomatoes from her one-tenth-acre plot and canned 512 number 3 cans of tomatoes. Her profit was $40.

All the while Marie continued to speak in schools around the state, organizing other clubs and requesting money for scholarships.

By now the General Education Board of New York City had contributed $25,000 and the United States Farm Demonstration Service $5,000 for canning machinery, but still there was no money for scholarships. Fall and tuition time for Katie sped closer. Since many wealthy Northerners wintered in Aiken, pretty Marie donned her best dress and called on some of these persons for financial assistance. Thomas Hitchcock answered her plea. The day Marie arrived home to find the letter confirming his contribution, she danced around the dining room of the boarding house and then sat down at the table and cried for joy.

Marie Cromer's Girls' Tomato Club attracted nationwide attention. The South Carolina legislature offered other scholarships, and word of the club spread. Within a year five other Southern states took up growing and canning tomatoes, and Marie's idea became a national movement fostered by the United States government.

Marie worked continually to improve the clubs by creating new learning experiences. She was now president of the Rural School Improvement Association of Aiken County and State Organizer of Tomato Clubs. In cooperation with the state of South Carolina, the United States Department of Agriculture appointed her an agent of the department on August 16, 1910.

On April 24, 1912, Marie married Superintendent Seigler. With the births of Cecil, Jr., and Rena Chaffee (later Mrs. Rena C. Seigler Snapp of Savannah, Georgia), she turned more to the duties of home. Her dream had been realized: not only had the clubs drawn the rural girls closer together, they had brought about reforms in the economic life of the farm women as they sold surplus goods. More importantly, the organization of the clubs had promoted self-confidence. The program now expanded into other activities, including sewing, cooking, and animal care.

"The Tomato Club," said Marie, "does not simply stand for the raising of tomatoes but for lessons ethical and economical."

The 1915 December issue of *American Magazine* hailed Marie as the Joan of Arc of a crusade of Southern women in agriculture "for by means of Girls' Tomato Clubs she is teaching three thousand girls to become independent through growing and putting up vegetables."

In speaking to a 4-H rally in Columbia on October 19, 1938, Senator James F. Byrnes said, "The pioneer spirit of Mrs. Seigler has resulted in the organization of girls' clubs in every state of the union. That this young woman's efforts were the origin of the 4-H Clubs is a source of great pride to all South Carolinians."

Because of Marie Seigler's efforts, Home Demonstration work had its birth in Aiken County.

The Aiken School System gave Marie a diamond sunburst brooch in recognition of her services, and in 1953 at the national 4-H camp in Washington, D.C., President Dwight E. Eisenhower presented her with a gold medallion honoring her for outstanding service to the nation.

In 1985 the Abbeville Chamber of Commerce and the Abbeville County Hall of Fame honored her further. A marker in the Abbeville County Educational Garden praises Marie and her work. A 1910 banner made by the Tomato Club hangs in the James Fell Log Cabin there.

Marie died June 14, 1964, and is buried in the Seigler family cemetery near Johnston, South Carolina.

Marie's dreams for making rural life more livable and fulfilling were clear in her letters to her Tomato Girls:

My dear Club Members,

We want efficient and contented girls in every home, and we have selected you to help demonstrate through your garden spot one way of helping to make a good home.

Every girl should help in the national demonstration work. We cannot afford to have a single member fail, and it is important that everyone should do her best. Of course you will be one of the best. Write us often for help and information about your garden work and do not fail to read carefully the enclosed instructions.

Marie Cromer
State Organizer

The motto of today's 4-H Club, "Make the best better," exemplifies the goal of Marie Samuella Cromer's vision put into practice through her Tomato Girls.

Elizabeth O'Neill Verner

ARTIST
1883–1979

Beth would never forget the grave faces of her parents and the kind bearded doctor who bent over her bed, their eyes gazing down in deep concern.

"The hip is dislocated," Dr. Simmons said, "and the bone diseased."

Mrs. O'Neill turned anxiously toward the doctor. "There must be some

Peck, Charleston *News and Courier*

treatment," she said. The family had lost a younger daughter from a similar illness. They could not bear to think they might lose another.

"A family in Chicago sent for a doctor from Austria to treat their child," Dr. Simmons told the parents. "I will go to Chicago to learn what that treatment is, if you are game to try it."

The treatment the doctor brought back involved long months in bed for Beth with weights attached to the afflicted leg.

At last he announced the bone healed. With prolonged treatment, the hip problem was corrected. Then Beth had to learn to walk again. Through her determination and diligence, she developed a beautiful carriage.

The O'Neill family engaged in many community activities in Charleston. Their large home on Friend Street, now 43 Legare, bustled with activity. Beth's mother, Molly, took time from her busy household to help found the auxiliary for Roper Hospital. She also founded the free kindergarten and did volunteer work in the schools. Beth's father, Henry, had been educated abroad, and now he worked as a rice broker. Both parents instilled their love of art, literature, and music in their children.

Beth's grandfathers also had a profound influence on her life. Grandfather Baker told her about his travels, showed her his souvenirs from Italy and France, and encouraged her to draw with tales of his days in art school. To Grandfather O'Neill, Beth always said, she owed her understanding of managing money.

Beth was educated in Catholic schools in Charleston. When her sister Flossie took art lessons with a young teacher, Miss Alice Ravenel Smith, Beth went along. She loved the lessons and Miss Smith and soon became her pupil too.

At fourteen Beth attended Ursuline Academy in Columbia. There she sang in the choir. Upon graduation she attended the Academy of Fine Arts in Philadelphia. She was especially pleased to go there, since it was Grandfather Baker's alma mater.

Back home in Charleston, she received invitations to visit old friends. It was during one of these visits to her Ursuline friends in Columbia that she met E. Pettigrew Verner. He and his brothers operated Verner Academy in the Verners' back yard on Senate Street. By teaching other boys, they were putting themselves through the University of South Carolina.

The O'Neill family experienced much sadness at the death of Henry O'Neill at the age of fifty-six. Molly was left with nine children. It became necessary for her to give up the house on Legare Street. She took in boarders and sold off property as money was needed.

In 1905 while Pettigrew Verner studied abroad, Beth taught for a year in Aiken. During this time they wrote to each other.

On his return, Beth was invited to visit the Verners' mountain home. The Verners, who were Protestant, expressed concern that the girl their son had chosen was high-spirited, "artistic," and Catholic. However, three years later when Pettigrew came to Charleston as a chemist, he and Beth were married.

The couple rented a small house at 19 Lamboll Street near where Beth had grown up. A year later their daughter Elizabeth was born. At this time Beth shared a studio with Leila Waring, the miniaturist, and continued her warm friendship with her one-time teacher, Alice Smith.

After a son, David, was born the Verners bought a house on 3 Atlantic Street. Young Mrs. Verner was an active wife and mother: she made her husband's shirts, painted oils and sold them at the Ladies' Exchange, and told stories at the Charleston Library.

After some emotional turmoil, Beth broke her ties with her church and became a Presbyterian with her husband's family. To lift her spirits about her own family's displeasure over her actions, Alice Smith involved her in new art techniques—woodblock printing and etching.

The Verners spent much of the hot summer months at the mountain house in North Carolina. It was during one of these times in 1925 that Pettigrew died quite suddenly after minor surgery.

Left with two children, a mortgage on their home, and little insurance, Beth faced the fact that she would have to make a living.

Encouraged by her brother, Harry, and by Alice Smith, she decided she could sell etchings—designs made by putting wax on a copper plate and drawing into it with a needle, thereby exposing the copper. The drawings had to be done in reverse. A room that had once been the nursery became her studio. Son David went with her to the museum to pull the press when she printed. Miss Alice sent Beth's work to shows with her own and directed buyers to her.

With hard work and the help of her son and daughter, honors began to come in for Beth. She was asked to exhibit her work and to lecture on art. In 1928 she demonstrated etching methods at the University of North Carolina, becoming the first woman to deliver a lecture there. She illustrated the Charleston edition of DuBose Heyward's *Porgy*. She also lectured at Randolph-Macon Woman's College. Such involvement led her to found the Southern States Art League.

By 1930 Beth had shown her work in Los Angeles, Brooklyn's Art Institute, the New School of Social Research in New York, the Arts and Crafts Society of New Orleans, and the Telfair in Savannah.

With daughter Betty accompanying her, she studied at the Central School of Arts in London. There she sketched constantly, even while the ship was unloading at Plymouth.

The two returned to Charleston to find America in the throes of the Depression. Only the wealthy still traveled and purchased drawings. These patrons kept Beth's studio open.

By now Rockefeller Center had purchased her drawings, the Metropolitan Museum had acquired her work for a print collection, and etchings had been filed in the Library of Congress in Washington—a first for a native South Carolinian.

In 1935 Elizabeth O'Neill Verner had a one-artist show in Boston. An artist who was showing at the same gallery warned her that her eyes would not be able to stand the strain of the fine lines of etching indefinitely and suggested Mrs. Verner try her medium—pastel. Beth found this new field exciting.

Ever since the days when Grandfather Baker told her of his travels, Beth had dreamed of a trip around the world. In 1937 she combined a visit to her sisters' homes in California and Hawaii, where her work was being exhibited, and the world tour. When, however, Beth and her travel companion, Emily Perry Brown, were crossing the Pacific, war broke out in Manchuria, and all plans had to be abandoned.

They did manage to reach Kyoto, where an artist taught her the Japanese brush stroke. She also etched wandering priests, market women, and Buddist monks.

In 1938 Beth moved her studio to 38 Tradd Street. It was here she found drawing on silk gave a permanence not found in most pastels. Later she drew on wood and her work gradually changed. Earlier she had done architectural subjects in both pencil and etchings, portraying the details of gates and brickwork.

With the pastels she did portraits of the flower sellers, countryside, great oaks, marshes, and shimmering beaches. Negroes with their beauty and dignity always delighted her. These delicate water-color sketches brought international acclaim.

In 1947 the Women's College of the University of North Carolina and the University of South Carolina awarded Mrs. Verner honorary degrees. In 1960 she was named to the Charleston Hall of Fame. In 1967 the College of Charleston gave her a doctorate of literature, and Governor Robert McNair took her Japanese etchings as a gift to the mayor of Kyoto.

Mrs. Verner was also the author of *Prints and Impressions of Charleston, Mellowed by Time,* and *The Stonewall Ladies.* She was the illustrator of a number of books. Before age slowed her activity, Mrs. Verner was active in the preservation of the Charleston she loved.

Always thrilling to the beauty of a tree or the sweep of the marshes, she told her students: "Think of God as an artist. He knows harmony, proportion and rhythm. The rainbow is His."

Mrs. Verner died on April 27, 1979, at ninety-five. She is buried in the graveyard of the First Scots Presbyterian Church at the corner of Tradd and Meeting streets beside her husband, Pettigrew. The Elizabeth O'Neill Verner Museum at 79 Church Street, adjacent to her former studio, houses her artwork.

Wil Lou Gray

EDUCATOR
1883–1984

"Wil Lou," her brother Dial said with a wink at his friend, "I'll give you a nickel if you won't talk for twenty minutes."

Wil Lou Gray twisted her fair-skinned face in thought and looked across their spacious porch in Laurens, South Carolina.

"I could do it," she thought, "if I just had something to keep in my mouth for that length of time. If only Papa would let me chew gum—but then of course he says that ladies don't chew—"

Suddenly Wil Lou stuck out her palm to her brother. "I'll do it!" she said.

With her five-cent piece in her pocket, she headed straight for the package of Brown Mule Chewing Tobacco she had seen stored among the woolen clothing to keep moths away.

After tearing off a plug and stuffing it in her mouth, she dashed back to the porch for the timing.

Unfortunately, the sick feeling that soon came from swallowing tobacco juice made the money hard to come by and taught Wil Lou a lesson as well.

It was difficult, however, for Wil Lou not to be doing something. Once a metalworker came to their home to install a grate for the fireplace, and the Gray children followed him to his shop. There they created eyeglasses and other objects with interesting shapes from the tin shavings.

Although her father blamed Dial for leading the others away from home, Wil Lou felt she had really been responsible.

Another matter about which William Lafayette Gray, a Christian gentleman of strong convictions, was strict was that of having no whiskey in his home except for a few drops on rock candy for a bad cough. However, on a trip to

South Caroliniana Library

New York, Mr. Gray heard that small doses of whiskey might help his wife, who had become an invalid.

In her usual manner of reasoning, Wil Lou came to the conclusion that if the whiskey was good for her mother, it would be good for her. Besides, she really wanted to know how it tasted.

One morning she slipped into the upstairs bedroom where her mother dozed in her high bed. She tiptoed around in the glow of the fire to the marble-top dresser with its lovely cut glass and bottles of medicine, eased the bottle down, and gulped.

Never had she felt such fire! Acting on impulse, she ran to the open fireplace and spat. The glowing coals caught up the alcohol and spat back at her. Luckily, the fire died down again, and Mrs. Gray was not awakened by her young daughter's commotion.

It was only the illness of her mother that marred her happy childhood memories, which included buying blocks of ice to churn ice cream and cracking nuts.

Because "Papa," as Wil Lou called her father, could not bring himself to tell Wil Lou that her mother, Sarah Lou Dial Gray, "couldn't live," he asked her uncle to do this for him.

At the age of nine, Wil Lou could not believe what she had heard. She took her cousin, son of the uncle who had given her the tragic news, and went into a back bedroom. Believing that God answers prayers, they knelt down and prayed that her mother would not be taken from them.

When Mrs. Gray died, Wil Lou came to the harsh realization that although God answered prayers, His will must be done. Thus, Wil Lou and her brothers were left with only the picture of a mother who was soft spoken, beauty loving, and kind.

For a while after her mother's death, Wil Lou and her brothers, Dial and Coke, went to live with an aunt and uncle. This uncle, Dr. Christopher, influenced Wil Lou to look for the best in life.

Some time later Mr. Gray married a young neighbor, whom the children had always loved dearly. Mary Dunklin, a teacher, loved her stepchildren, and they were considerate of her. The three Gray children returned to their home, which was later blessed with another girl and boy.

Being from a devout Methodist family, Wil Lou heard many missionaries speak while she was growing up. They inspired her to want to help others.

After graduating from Columbia College in 1903 and summer study at Winthrop, Wil Lou headed over muddy, country roads by horse and buggy toward her first teaching position in Greenwood County.

With brother Coke at the harness, Wil Lou chatted on happily until at sundown they finally pulled up to the white, two-story home of Dr. Jones, chairman of the school's board of trustees. She certainly would like it here.

Shortly, however, Wil Lou's chatter faded. Dr. Jones directed them to a tiny cottage down the road where his daughter, her husband, and their young son lived. Wil Lou's heart fell to her high-buttoned shoes.

"Oh, I mustn't show my disappointment," she breathed to herself, for Wil Lou was always thoughtful of others.

But once she was admitted to the shining cleanliness of the house, her spirits lifted. The chimney of the freshly filled kerosene lamp was smoke-free, and the coverlet on the plump feather mattress was spotless.

The next day back at home at the dinner table, Coke told their family, "Wil

Lou will never stay. There is no place to sit in the house except in the kitchen or the bedroom And—," he blushed before he added, "there isn't even a privy—inside or out."

But Wil Lou did stay. She had been taught to call on the Lord in time of need, and now she dropped to her knees in front of the washstand in her small bedroom. "Lord," she prayed, "I can't do this by myself, and I don't know much about teaching, but give me the strength to stick it out and do my best for the children."

Indeed, she did do her best. Immediately accepted for her youthfulness and friendliness, she became involved in all phases of the community life. She even withstood the blow that in her position as a teacher she was expected to be there to celebrate Christmas with her students.

In her one-room school, Wil Lou had pupils of all ages. Here she tried every type of teaching, often writing her own material. One of the projects most enthusiastically undertaken was that of making maps from paper-maché. The students stayed after school to work on the maps until parents complained that their children were spending too much time at school.

As Miss Gray continued her work in education, she saw a sight that made a deep impression on her: a white tenant farmer who signed with a mark because he could not write his name.

Now a supervisor of rural schools in Laurens County, she organized the first rural night school in South Carolina. Yet she was disappointed in the lack of support she received in her efforts to teach adults to read and write. Consequently, she took a job in Maryland.

After continuing her education at Vanderbilt and receiving a master's degree in political science from Columbia University in New York, Wil Lou returned to South Carolina. In 1918 she was made executive secretary of the South Carolina Illiteracy Commission. Under the influence of this organization, the General Assembly established a department of adult education with Miss Gray as supervisor. Thus, through rain, cold, and hub-deep mud, she traveled over the state organizing schools for adults who had not had the opportunity for an education.

In her travels she urged mill presidents to employ teachers. She organized schools for adults in tobacco barns with flickering lanterns. Many of her teachers served without pay to teach people who were hungry to learn but did not want it known they could not read.

In 1923 a "Write Your Name" campaign helped organize many more adult schools.

One of her male students, who drove other adults to the school in his wagon, made all her struggles worthwhile when he said, "I would gladly give half of my crop this year if I could learn to read and write."

The night schools and her work with blacks did much to promote racial understanding in South Carolina.

Since there were no books that would make interesting reading for beginning adult readers, Miss Gray wrote her own. Some dealt with health and good manners, for Miss Gray believed that good citizenship should begin with a person's pride in his appearance.

At first, day school for adults was held only in summer. Miss Gray used a DAR school at Tamassee to offer poor women who worked in textile mills an opportunity to complete their educations. Later the campuses of South Carolina colleges served.

Although Miss Gray bubbled with inner happiness over the success of her part-time educational program, the desire for a year-round program burned within her. She talked to everyone about it and led a crusade for legislative approval and assistance. One senator said of Miss Gray, "She is worse than chewing gum in your hair."

For twenty-five years Miss Gray fought for her dream of a continuing school. It was in this spirit that she fulfilled her dream—the Opportunity School in West Columbia, the only one of its kind in the United States. The only requirements for entry were that the applicant be over sixteen, have good morals, and a desire to learn. The school opened in the hospital area of a former World War II Army Air Base.

This school, with its strong individualized approach, gave many a second chance. Letters still come from former students. One said, "You have to be at the Opportunity School only a few days before you catch the wonderful spirit—the spirit of friendship, loyalty, and accomplishment." Some graduates have gone on to college and to become leaders in their communities.

Among Miss Gray's major accomplishments during this time were her sightseeing trips or "pilgrimages," as she called them. She wanted her students to know their state and nation. These tours furnished much lasting joy.

Upon retirement she was appointed director of the Senior Citizens of America. She organized a state chapter which led to the formation of the Interagency Council on Aging.

At the age of ninety-four Miss Wil Lou was instrumental in the design of a game, "Palmetto Patriots," with proceeds going to Opportunity School scholarships.

Miss Gray's unselfish service to others has been rewarded in many ways. Winthrop and Columbia colleges bestowed honorary degrees upon her. Besides her honorary degree from Columbia College, she received their first Distinguished Service Award, and more recently the Alumnae Association's Distinguished Service Award. Wofford College also awarded her a doctorate of letters, the first honorary degree given to a woman.

In 1971 President Richard Nixon signed the Algernon Sydney Sullivan Award, which she received "in recognition of exceptional service to others in the finest American tradition."

Honors in 1974 included a tribute from the South Carolina General Assembly and induction into the South Carolina Hall of Fame.

In addition to scholastic honors, Dr. Gray was recognized by the Pilot Club, the Rotary Club, *Progressive Farmer Magazine,* the State American Legion, South Carolina State College, the Council of Common Good, Delta Kappa

Sandlapper Magazine

Gamma Society of South Carolina, the National Retired Teachers' Association, the Sertoma International, Status of Women Conference, Vocational Rehabilitation, the State Department of Education, and even Bob Hope. Columbia TV station WIS and Union Oil Company named her the "Spirit of '76."

Dr. Gray served on many boards, bringing to them her understanding of public affairs and the needs of people.

In receiving all these honors and having the Opportunity School renamed for her, Miss Wil Lou remarked, "The honors are not for me but for my coworkers, teachers, pupils, and friends."

Miss Wil Lou was the subject of many articles and wrote or assisted in compiling many books.

Throughout her distinguished career, Dr. Gray turned obstacles into stepping stones. Her ability to combine her faith in people with hard work made her a trailblazer in the field of education. As her Sullivan Award reads: "She held out her hands to her fellowman."

This pioneer for adult education died on March 10, 1984. She was a member of Washington Street Methodist Church. She is buried in Laurens.

Lily Strickland

COMPOSER
1884–1958

Lazy Southern days with their magic of cotton fields, magnolias, and mocking birds cast a spell over Echo Hall in Anderson, South Carolina, the day Lily Strickland was born.

It is no wonder that Lily reached for the piano keys on her tiptoes, for music filled her early years. Rhythm and melody swept over her as she sat at the edge of the cotton fields listening to the black pickers singing at their work and making up songs as they went along. Too, her grandfather, Judge J. Pinckney Reed, sang her to sleep.

Lily's family made their home at Echo Hall until her father's business took them to New York City. After the death of her father, Charlton Hines Strickland, Lily, along with her mother and two brothers, returned to the home of her maternal grandparents.

Encouraged by her family and particularly by an older cousin, Reed Miller— himself a concert tenor—Lily played the piano and wrote music as early as age nine. She played the pipe organ in the Episcopal Church and at sixteen published her first song.

After being tutored at home, her first formal education began at Converse College in Spartanburg, South Carolina, when she was eighteen. Five years later a scholarship to the Institute of Musical Art, a part of the Juilliard School of Music in New York, gave her the opportunity to study piano, orchestration, and composition. She and her mother took an apartment in New York. Much to Lily's delight, she found one of her teachers was using a composition of hers as a model for his other students.

One day as her mother attempted to enter their apartment, the door stuck. Mrs. Strickland asked assistance from a Columbia University graduate student who lived in the same building. As they entered the apartment, Lily was playing the piano. A friendship was begun. Lily learned the young man was Joseph Courtney Anderson, a South Carolinian and teacher at Columbia University.

In 1912 they were married. When Joseph accepted a job as education director of Camp MacArthur in Waco, Texas, Lily served as a volunteer entertainer for the Y.M.C.A. Her composing continued with wartime songs such as "America Victorious" and "To Our Allied Dead."

Around 1915 Lily's creations began to show the influence of her Southern upbringing. Songs with black dialect like "Honey Chile," "Pickaninny Sleep Song," and "Heah Dem Bells" began to receive the attention of the public.

Further travels through the southwestern part of the United States inspired other compositions with American Indian and Mexican highlights.

In 1920 when Lily followed her husband to his new business position in

India, she delved into the culture of that country and the surrounding ones. Finding the music and dances of India to be profound expressions of the oriental spiritual life touched Lily deeply. In sympathy and sensitivity to their powerful interpretations, she drew new life from their drum beats into her own music. Her years in the Far East were creative; there she composed music such as the "Oasis Suite." From piano suites to music for dancers and articles on the native customs, Lily strove to show how vital music is in oriental culture.

Though Lily appeared outwardly unconcerned with the discrimination manifested against women composers at this time, she did on occasion use a male pseudonym. She also used her mother's name spelled backward—Aseret Dnommah—to create the impression that "A Beggar at Love's Gate" was written by an Indian.

In 1924 Converse College bestowed a doctor of music degree on Lily. Her songs were becoming famous. "Mah Lindy Lou" had become a folk song with its lilting and haunting melody of a mockingbird.

Honey, did you heah dat mockin'bird sing las' night?
O Lawd, he wuz singing' sweet in de moonlight.

Blessed with a marvelous sense of humor, which was often characterized by a twinkle in her eyes, Lily liked to tell of hearing a prima donna abroad sing "Mah Lindy Lou" by imposing an Italian accent upon the Negro dialect.

In 1930 the couple returned to America, where they lived in Woodstock in the Catskill Mountains. Later they made Great Neck, Long Island, their home. In 1942 they spent eight months in Charleston, South Carolina, where Joseph set up a USO Club. Charleston made a deep impression, resulting in Lily's writing "Charleston Sketches." The six-part orchestral suite included "The Bells of Saint Michael's" and "On the Battery."

Much of Lily's work was uplifting as well as entertaining. Churches widely use her oratorio "Saint John the Beloved" and the cantatas "Star Over Bethlehem" and "The Song of David."

As an early twentieth-century artist, Lily Strickland's contribution to the field of music education was invaluable. In articles she expressed the need for developing creativity in children and particularly stressed the value of music in the home and in school. She composed volumes of songs for children as well as operettas, pantomimes, and dances.

In 1948 the composer and her husband retired to a home in the Blue Ridge Mountains near Hendersonville, where she continued to write until her death on June 6, 1958.

A person of tireless energy, Lily Strickland was also regarded as a poet, having written sonnets and many of the lyrics for the songs. Her articles were published in scholarly journals. A talented artist, she illustrated the covers for many of her songs and sketched and painted in water colors.

At the time of Lily's death, companies had published 395 of her compositions, as well as music composed for the Ziegfeld Follies and other well-known dance groups.

With a heart and mind attuned to the rhythm and beauty of life, Lily Strickland made an enduring contribution to the world of music. She is buried in Anderson in Old Silverbrook Cemetery beside her husband. Her tombstone reads, "He put a song in my heart."

Sandlapper Magazine

Mary Gordon Ellis

SENATOR
1890–1934

The year was 1924. Mary Gordon Ellis, superintendent of Jasper County schools, made every minute count. She *would* have an exemplary school program for blacks and whites.

As a teacher-principal of Gillisonville School some years earlier, she had known firsthand of the appalling conditions of the county schools. When her own children had become school age, she refused to send them to the inadequate schools of Jasper County. Instead, she boarded them with relatives in Savannah in order to have them participate in a better educational program.

Now as superintendent she set about upgrading the Low Country school

South Caroliniana Library

system. She began by closing numerous small schools and consolidating the county into five districts with a representative from each district. She worked toward building a teacherage to attract better instructors. She initiated in-service programs for further teacher training.

Much to the disapproval of some white citizens in the county, Mrs. Ellis insisted that black children should be provided bus transportation just as whites were. Part of her campaign to upgrade the black schools included getting new books without missing pages rather than the hand-me-downs from the white schools. She also hired Mary Alice Miller, a black university graduate, to supervise the black schools.

When a Julius Rosenwald fund became available to build black schools in the South, Mrs. Ellis organized benefits and ice cream suppers to provide the matching funds for eligibility.

Local citizens who felt her measures had gone too far—particularly in the black schools—pressed their Jasper County House member, H.K. Purdy, to do something about her. As a result, Representative Purdy wrote Mrs. Ellis that she was fired.

Mrs. Ellis faced the representative with determination. "Not only will I not retire," she told him, "but I will oppose you in the next election."

When, in the summer of 1928, she learned Purdy had filed for the South Carolina Senate, she hurried to the courthouse and filed for the same seat. Political meetings, like the work in the schools, became a family affair. When the election date rolled around, the vote was a tie, but the run-off proved Mary Gordon Ellis a winner.

With her election came a new problem—one laced with a bit of humor. Never before had a woman become a senator; consequently, the men in the Senate chamber did not know how to address her. Should there be, they wondered, a feminine form for *senator*? Close associates solved the dilemma by calling her Mary G.

The manner in which she was addressed bothered Mary Ellis no more than the talk of whether or not she would wear a hat in the Senate chamber. She had run for office to take care of business, and that she did. Records show she debated, proposed bills, made amendments, and served on committees during the 1929–1932 sessions.

Working to reach her goals was nothing new to Mrs. Ellis, born Mary Gordon on April 21, 1890, in Gourdin, South Carolina. One of ten children of Alexander M. and Mary Gamble Gordon, Sr., Mary knew her future rested on her own shoulders. Though she was not yet sure just what that future would be, she was always eager to learn. At one time the family missed the teen-ager, only to find her scrunched down in the back of the Williamsburg County courthouse listening to the workings of the law.

After graduation from Kingstree High School in 1909, Mary taught at Sutton's School for a year. Few rural schools in South Carolina had teachers with college degrees, but Mary was determined she would get the qualified training needed for teaching.

With a scholarship to serve tables in the dining room, she enrolled in Winthrop College, where she earned an A.B. degree in 1913.

It was during her first year of teaching at Gillisonville School that Mary met and married Junius Gather Ellis, a farmer and turpentine operator of Coosawatchee.

The couple had three children, Mary Elizabeth, Margaret Lee, and Junius Gather. Always energetic, Mary took care of her family, performed the household duties, and kept books for her husband. During these years, she never lost her belief in the value of a good education for South Carolina's school children. When her own children were older, she took the opportunity to do something about her concerns. Eventually she became the first woman ever to serve in the general assembly of South Carolina.

Although Mary Ellis worked hard outside her home to improve education, a daughter remembers her mother sewing, canning, gardening, and even butchering.

Mrs. Ellis had strong convictions about what a home should be. She expressed these opinions in a courthouse address in Columbia on March 27, 1930. "The influence of the home," she said, "stands by the child when he grows up and determines whether he makes a good citizen or a poor one. The whole nation goes back to the home."

After the death of her father and as her own health failed, Mrs. Ellis was no longer physically able to campaign for re-election. As a result, she did not retain her post. After a lengthy battle with cancer, this senator and champion educator died in 1934. She is buried in Williamsburg Cemetery at Kingstree.

Mary C. Simms Oliphant

HISTORIAN
1891–1988

A sixth grader in Barnwell knew there was something different about their petite substitute teacher who was teaching while at home on a break from college. Before long, he found out what it was—she "loved" the South Carolina history she was teaching his class. What the sixth grader could not know was that this pretty, brown-haired lady, who made the people and places of her beloved state live for him, would one day affect millions of other school children over South Carolina.

May, as she was affectionately called, once said, "I was born loving history." With William Gilmore Simms for a grandfather, that was not surprising. Although she never knew this nineteenth-century novelist, historian, and poet except through his children and his books, he greatly influenced her life.

Born in Barnwell to William Gilmore and Emma Gertrude Hartzog Simms, this third daughter and sixth child was christened Mary Chevillette Simms. Mary's middle name is evidence of her family's loyalty and interest in preservation. When an ancestor's husband, whose name was Chevillette, grieved because he had no children to carry on his name in America, his wife's family promised that someone in every generation of their family would bear his name. Mary's middle name helped to fulfill that promise. She proudly bore the name of Chevillette, never failing to sign her name with the C.

Mary C. Simms attended the College for Women in Columbia, where she graduated in 1916 with a degree in liberal arts and piano. A week after graduation she was approached about updating her grandfather's 1840 *History of South Carolina* for use as a textbook in the schools. Just as William Gilmore Simms's daughter, Augusta, and other children had been the inspiration for his history, Mrs. Oliphant's desire to share her love of her state with the school children of South Carolina spurred her to take up the challenge.

The following March of 1917, Miss Simms and Albert Drane Oliphant were

Family Photo

married. When Mrs. Oliphant's South Carolina history manuscript was completed, she was faced with the task of getting the approval of the state board of education for its adoption for classroom use. Fully aware of the status of women in a society that did not yet allow her sex to vote, Mrs. Mary Chevillette Simms Oliphant appeared before the board. In her stylishly simple dress and hat, she spoke on behalf of her book. Although Mrs. Oliphant was only four feet, five inches tall, her commanding presence and persuasive speech won the adoption for the upcoming five-year period. Thus, her work of love filled the need for making young people aware of their heritage and environment.

With this publication, Mrs. Oliphant launched her writing career. She continued to update her grandfather's history until 1932, when she ventured out to write her own.

In the early years of their marriage, the Oliphants moved to Greenville, where Albert Oliphant was southern editor of *Textile World* magazine. When McGraw-Hill bought the company, he became southern manager for that firm. The couple had three children: Mary Simms, Albert Drane, Jr., and William Gilmore Simms.

During the ensuing years Mrs. Oliphant's name became synonymous with South Carolina history. Many adults recall studying *The South Carolina Reader*, written in 1927 to accompany the South Carolina history, or *Gateway to South Carolina*, a third-grade reader written with her daughter, Mrs. Alester G. Furman III, in 1947. In the latter book, students accompany Mary and Albert

Family Photo

on their adventures with their enthusiastic teacher, Miss Hattie. In doing so, they learn about the American Indian and nature, as well as the state's heroes and its history. Miss Hattie is ever ready for a field trip or a tour, especially to the woods she loves. And then there's the verse of poetry always on the tip of Miss Hattie's tongue or the song "Carolina" to instill pride. This book evolved over the years into a social studies text called *South Carolina—From the Mountains to the Sea*, which is still studied in the South Carolina schools.

From 1917 to 1977 there were nine editions of Mrs. Oliphant's history, which was studied in the South Carolina schools for sixty-seven years. A tricentennial edition was the first to be co-authored with her daughter. A son, Simms, also assisted in some of the updating and revising of the histories.

An even more ambitious task than the writing of her histories were Mrs. Oliphant's editing of her grandfather's letters. The monumental project, of which she was co-editor, proved to be a six-volume collection rich in information on Southern life and literature. Her other works include the editing of *The Centennial Edition of the Writings of William Gilmore Simms*, of which *Voltmeier, or the Mountain Men* was the first volume to be printed.

Among Mrs. Oliphant's other writings are a catalogue of the *Works of A.S. Salley* and two school workbooks. Her total publishings exceed twenty volumes.

Throughout Mrs. Oliphant's life she was deeply involved in collecting and preserving history. Though the Civil War had destroyed the original house, it gave her great pleasure to be able to have Woodlands, her ancestral home, designated as a National Historic Landmark. The family plantation south of Bamberg on the Edisto River was always a place of spiritual strength for her. The descendants of William Gilmore Simms still enjoy visits to Woodlands, with its walking paths through moss-hung oaks.

Always generous with her time in assisting others working in Southern literature and history, Mrs. Oliphant made countless contributions to the state. She was widely known as an eloquent speaker and often called upon to pay tribute to other deserving South Carolinians.

As a result of her historical research, Mrs. Oliphant was named director of the state library association. She received an Award of Merit from the American Association of State and Local History in 1964 and an honorary degree from the University of South Carolina. Furman University gave her an honorary membership in Phi Beta Kappa.

Mrs. Oliphant was one of the first honorary members of the Delta Kappa Gamma Society for teachers. In 1983 she was inducted into the South Carolina Hall of Fame. The state's highest honor, the Palmetto Award, was bestowed upon her in 1980.

Mary Chevillette Simms Oliphant died at the age of ninety-seven on July 27, 1988. She was buried at Holy Apostle's Episcopal Church in Barnwell near others of the Simms family. Her tombstone bears her grandfather's motto, *Video Volans:* "Soaring, I See." Indeed, this mother, historian, speaker, and friend would have made her grandfather proud.

Anne Austin Young

PIONEER WOMAN DOCTOR
1892–1989

A Thanksgiving moon danced eerily over tombs in the cemetery near the Nurses Training School of the University of Maryland, but Anne Austin and her friends didn't mind. Anne's mother had sent a box of home-cooked food all the way from Cross Hill, South Carolina, and spunky Anne was determined to share it with her medical student friends, Henry and Mason Young.

Never mind that strict rules governing student nurses in 1910 forbade being with male students. Nobody would detect them in the cemetery having a picnic on the marble slab marking Edgar Allan Poe's grave.

Only such escapades made nursing school bearable for Anne. From 7 A.M. to 7 P.M. she cared for patients in the hospital ward, scrubbed floors, and washed windows. In the evening she attended classes until 10 P.M. Besides having such a rigorous schedule, student nurses endured most unprofessional treatment. When a doctor came on the nursing floor, they were not allowed to speak unless they were spoken to. Anyone dating an intern was expelled.

As Anne stood by watching doctors attend patients, she found herself longing to be in their shoes. Her heart's desire had been to study medicine—even if it was a man's profession. But finances made her dream impossible. Consequently, she had enrolled in the Nurses Training School, and she would stick it out.

The Austins of Cross Hill had been leaders in their community since 1804, when Anne's great grandparents came from Ireland in search of religious freedom. Thrifty, hard-working people, they had always lived close to God and the land. Anne's grandfather, Robert Campbell Austin, was a doctor at Cross Hill. Her father, Robert Alexander Austin, was a surveyor, a merchant, and later a funeral director.

In 1887 he married Clara Nabers, and they had two daughters, Katy and Anne. Anne was born on January 15, 1892, three years after her sister's birth. The family attended Liberty Springs Presbyterian Church where Ann Pamela Cunningham's family worshiped.

The sisters loved the long summer days on the farm. They played jump rope and hopscotch under the shade of the big water oaks, built dams across the farm streams, dug up quartz rocks near the springhouse, and tobogganed down the hill over a carpet of pine needles. If their father was working in the fields, they liked taking him water in a gourd dipper.

Admittedly, Anne with her vivid imagination and precociousness, thought up mischief for the sisters to get into. Once as they played around the "coffin house," they climbed into one of the wooden boxes. Much to their surprise, Uncle Willie, who was in partnership with Anne's father, began hammering on the lid.

Though Anne sometimes tested her parents' patience, they knew her to be an independent spirit who was loving and tenderhearted and quick to make amends for her transgressions.

Evenings found the family gathered to listen to Mr. Austin read from the Bible.

Mrs. Austin tutored the girls at home, and when Anne was eight, the sisters entered third grade at Cross Hill. The school had several grades in one class. Along with their studies, the teacher placed emphasis on memory work and recitation.

Impressed by hearing a missionary from China tell about the Chinese buildings with turned-up eaves that let evil spirits slide off, Anne wrote a paper about it. Her essay won a contest and was published in *The Laurens Advertiser.*

Family Photo

Anne Austin on the day she received her degree in medicine

In 1906 Anne entered Presbyterian College, fourteen miles away. By now she had developed into a pretty young woman with a slender, graceful figure and a twenty-two-inch waistline. Although she studied diligently and made high grades, she was always ready for fun. The college offered much in extracurricular activities, but the glee club and declamation contests were closed to girls. It was not considered proper for them to speak in public.

While Anne was a student at Presbyterian College, she met a young local dentist, Henry Young. A tall, lanky fellow from Due West, he was always laughing, whistling, or telling jokes. He filled a tooth for Anne when she went home to Cross Hill, and she learned he had become a friend of her family. Since he was eight years older, the thought of dating him never entered her mind. Later, however, they studied in the same school.

When Anne finished college at the top of her class, officials found themselves in a dilemma. The valedictorian had always been male. A woman, they thought, should not be in the spotlight. After much discussion and painful soul-searching, those in charge allowed Anne to deliver the address in the graduating exercises.

In addition to graduating magna cum laude, Anne received the South Carolina history medal, a Bible medal, and an English essay award. She was eighteen.

Back home at Cross Hill Anne shocked her family by announcing, "I want to be a doctor."

"Just put your foot down and hear no more about it," her Uncle Willie said to the Austins. "Women are not meant to be doctors. If she's interested in the medical field, she can be a nurse."

But convinced of their daughter's seriousness, Anne's parents stood behind her. Yet they could not afford to send her to medical school.

Anne did go into nursing but only as a stopgap on the way to reaching her real goal. After completing her training and passing the exam, she decided against working the long duty hours required before a salary began. Instead, she passed the teachers' exam and began teaching in a one-room school near her home. She taught all nine grades. After paying her room and board in a nearby farmhouse, she set aside the rest of her money for medical school. At night she studied medical books by the light of a kerosene lamp.

During this time Anne spent weekends with her family. Near the Austin farm were black children who did not attend church. When Anne organized a Sunday School class for them, she was criticized by the father of one of the white pupils in her school.

"If your daughter doesn't stop what she's doing," he told Anne's father, "I will take my child out of her class."

Mr. Austin, ordinarily a mild-mannered man, replied, "Anne will do what she wants to do, and neither you or anyone else will tell her how to live her life."

In September of 1911 Anne eagerly boarded a Seaboard train for the Woman's Medical College of Pennsylvania. There she worked part-time in the laboratory and set up a typing service to help pay her expenses. In spite of the rigid

Family Photo

Dr. Anne Austin Young and her husband, Dr. Henry Young

schedule, she never missed a day of class. When the going got rough, she drew on her sense of humor to keep plugging away. Her top scholastic standing won her a scholarship each year.

A requirement before taking senior classes was delivering twenty babies. Medical students met this requirement in the slums of Philadelphia. One of the immigrant mothers Anne attended gave her a lace collar, which she wore on her graduation gown.

At the ceremonies in 1915 Anne had to pinch herself to make sure she was not dreaming—a little country girl from South Carolina was top honor graduate of the Woman's Medical College.

After receiving her degree, Anne became the only woman on a staff of fourteen at what is now the South Carolina State Hospital in Columbia. Even though she found the job demanding, Anne felt it was all worthwhile every time one of her patients improved enough to rejoin his family.

It worried Anne that mentally retarded patients were placed in the hospital with mentally ill patients. Many of the mentally handicapped, she felt, could be helped with the right kind of environment. She worked toward legislation to make her dream come true. Whitten Village in Clinton came into being largely through her efforts.

While she was at State Hospital, Anne bought a Model-T Ford and out of necessity learned to change a tire and tinker with the motor.

Anne had continued her friendship with the young dentist, now a medical doctor in Anderson. On Easter, March 31, 1918, she married Dr. Charles Henry Young. They spent their honeymoon attending a course at the Mayo Clinic in Minnesota. In addition to their love for each other, they shared a love of medicine. For many years they spent every summer vacation at famous medical clinics. They worked as a team in their work as well as in giving to missions. Of all their accomplishments, giving birth to their daughter Anne was most meaningful.

This pioneer woman doctor, who entered the medical profession when it was considered improper for a woman to do so, was honored by Governor James B. Edwards in 1977. She received the Service Award to Mankind from the Anderson County Medical Society, as well as from Sertoma Club International. Presbyterian College in Clinton awarded her the Gold P Award, and Anderson County Mental Health Association bestowed the Service to the Mentally Retarded Award upon her. In 1981 she was inducted into the South Carolina Hall of Fame. She was awarded an honorary doctorate degree from Columbia College.

Dr. Young died on January 25, 1989, twenty-one years after the death of her husband. She is buried at Forest Lawn Memorial Park in Anderson. She was ninety-seven. She is survived by her daughter, Mrs. Anne Sweetman of Anderson, as well as grandchildren.

Elizabeth White

ARTIST
1893–1976

When Elizabeth White's grandfather gave her a box of water colors at the age of four, he sparked an interest that would last throughout her life. She never dreamed, however, that what she did out of her love for art would one day make her famous. Because Elizabeth painted only for the pleasure it gave, she never thought of signing or dating her creations.

At the age of seven, Elizabeth lost her mother, Elizabeth Howard White. Several years later her father, William, died. An only child, Elizabeth lived with her grandparents, Anthony and Elizabeth Dick White. Her grandfather was a lawyer and a Sumter County farmer. He served in the state legislature and founded the Sumter Insurance Company, where Elizabeth's father had worked. An aunt also lovingly cared for Elizabeth in the Sumter home.

As she grew older, there was never any pressure on Elizabeth to one day pursue her art for profit. Yet she did have a driving force within her—the desire to do her very best in her work. Any work of art, she felt, must follow basic rules and traditions set by experienced artists of the past. Combined with this study and practice of the art, she said, must come discipline.

It was this philosophy that led Elizabeth to pursue her formal education at the Columbia College for Women, where she received a certificate in art. She continued her study at the Pennsylvania Academy of Fine arts in Philadelphia, one of the oldest art schools in America. It was there that art really came alive for Elizabeth. Studying under instructors whom she admired was a treasured

South Caroliniana Library

experience for her.

In her work with oils, Miss White became particularly adept in capturing the likenesses of people. The facial expressions of the Negroes she painted show a depth of feeling. In the portraits of elderly blacks they are presented with dignity against familiar Southern backgrounds.

Elizabeth's favorite work with the theme of the Southern black was her pencil sketch of her beloved servant, Elizabeth Brown, who dedicated more than forty years to caring for members of the White family. The artist was always quick to give much of the credit for her success to the loyal friendship and love of "Lizzie."

Having spent a portion of each year at Pawley's Island and in the North Carolina mountains, Miss White also drew heavily on that scenery for her painting. Touring Europe with a friend and the friend's father also allowed her to paint in other locations—especially France. Visiting museums gave new insights and further developed her talents.

When, along with other artists, she received an invitation to study and paint at the Tiffany Foundation at Oyster Bay, Long Island, Miss White was able to paint in still other beautiful surroundings. A flower study she painted there won a prize in Houston, Texas.

An even more prestigious honor came when Miss White was invited to come to the MacDowell Colony in New Hampshire. In this retreat, where serious artists before her had come to allow their creativity to reach its height, Miss White produced some of her best work. One of her paintings of the trees surrounding the Colony was purchased by the Library of Congress.

Miss White learned she had received the invitation to come to the Colony based on her pen and ink postcards of South Carolina. The wife of the sanctuary's founder had been captivated by Miss White's postcard drawings of Sumter's Swan lake, the stately old churches, the beaches, and countless other scenes with moss-strewn oaks.

Perhaps Miss White is best known for her etchings. Her diligence in spending many hours in study and preparation before attempting the difficult task of producing a design on metal or glass paid off. "It looks so easy," she once said, "that people have a tendency to think there's nothing to it." Miss White's etching "All God's Chillun Got Wings"—inspired by a church scene—was chosen to represent South Carolina at the New York World's Fair.

The stimulation of studying under renowned teachers had always been relished by the artist. Thus, when the chance came to study under such renowned artists as Wayman Adams of New York and Alfred Hutty of Charleston, Miss White again acted on her belief in learning all she could about her art.

During her earlier years, Miss White also taught—first in the Sumter schools and then as instructor in art at the University of South Carolina.

Miss White's drawings appeared as illustrations in several books. Her works have been exhibited in the Smithsonian Print Gallery in Washington, the

South Caroliniana Library

Philadelphia Exhibit of Art, the Tiffany Foundation in New York, and the Southern Art League, as well as in the Gibbes Art Gallery in Charleston, Duke University, Mint Museum in Charlotte, the Columbia Museum of Art, and the Sumter Gallery of Art.

The artist was an active member of the Sumter Art Association and co-organizer of the Artists' Guild. She was a charter member of the Sumter County Historical Association and the Pilots International.

Upon Miss White's death in 1976, her Sumter home on 421 North Main Street was used as she requested: "in a manner that will promote the natural beauty of the property, promote the arts, and be a place of enjoyment to the public." The grandfather's home, where the artist was born and did much of her work, is now the Sumter Gallery of Art. It exhibits paintings and etchings by the artist. Often called the "Elizabeth White House," it is on the National Register of Historic Places.

Nell Graydon

AUTHOR, PRESERVATIONIST
1893–1986

Nell Graydon yanked her fishing line from the foamy surf, moved along Edisto beach, and flung it out again not far from her husband's.

"You know why you don't catch any fish?" Sterling asked with a twinkle in his eyes. "You don't leave your hook in one place long enough for the fish to find it."

Family Photo

Mrs. Graydon's fishing attempts characterized her eagerness "to get on with" any task she tackled, whether it was collecting tales from the coastal marshes or preserving some historical landmark.

Even though Mrs. Graydon's writing wasn't begun until much later in life—after her children were grown and her husband had retired from his presidency of a brick manufacturing plant—she had always loved to read. And her somewhat solitary youth allowed time for daydreaming—perhaps the stirrings of a future author.

Born in Pineville, North Carolina, to A.B. and Margaret Eleanor Wilson Saunders, Nell lost her mother when she was three years old. Her mother's unmarried sister came to "look after" the family. "Sister," as they called her, performed her duty as best she knew how in her prim and proper way. Nell remembered long hours under Sister's watchful eye—hours she spent sitting on their front porch looking at magazines or lost in thought.

When Nell was sixteen, her father remarried. Nell's association with her stepmother was a pleasant one. She enjoyed visiting her stepmother's family in Mississippi, and their friendship lasted through the years.

After graduating from Elizabeth College in Charlotte, North Carolina, where she majored in English and drama, Nell married Sterling Graydon. A native of Abbeville, South Carolina, Sterling had come to Charlotte to work with his uncle.

In 1930 the couple moved to Greenwood, South Carolina, to make their home. The family was blessed with three children: Virginia, Sterling, and Frank.

When the Graydons acquired a summer home on Edisto Island, Nell was charmed by the area—stretches of tidal marshes, sea grass along the salt creeks and inlets, and great live oaks shrouded in moss. But most of all, she was fascinated by the people of the island and the stories they had to tell.

Islanders welcomed Mrs. Graydon into their homes and invited her to look through family albums and other items stored away in musty old trunks. Threading the history and character of these people into stories, she pulled her listeners into their world.

When friends encouraged her to submit her stories for publication, she sent them to *The State Magazine.* Thus, the stories of Edisto launched her writing career.

Other newspapers published her works, and in 1955 her stories were collected into her first volume, *Tales of Edisto,* to be followed by *Another Jezebel,* the story of a glamorous spy of the Civil War. This historical fiction was based on a real person, Amelia Burton Boozer Feaster. Next came *Tales of Beaufort* and *Tales of Columbia.* Always in her stories she sought out the less-known incidents to share with her growing readership.

In 1965 Mrs. Graydon found a packet of ribbon-tied letters in a desk purchased when the Hofmann home in Aiken was being dismantled. The letters had been written to Marie Hofmann by her husband, Josef. Mrs. Graydon received the blessings of the Hofmann children to tell their famous father's story. Josefa and George turned over to Mrs. Graydon a trunk filled with journals, clippings, and photographs. As co-author, she wrote *The Amazing Marriage of Marie Eustis and Josef Hofmann.* She also co-authored *The McKissicks of South Carolina.*

Eliza of Wappoo, the story of Eliza Lucas Pinckney, who introduced indigo to South Carolina, was published in 1967.

In a deviation from her historical novels and folklore, Mrs. Graydon next published a cookbook, *From My House to Your House. South Carolina Ghost Tales* and *South Carolina Gardens* followed in 1971 and 1973.

Throughout her long-running romance with South Carolina, Mrs. Graydon always said, "I look upon my writing as a hobby."

Along with her driving concern to preserve the lore of her adopted state was the compulsion to restore historical landmarks, such as the Masonic Female College at Cokesbury in Greenwood County. Although Mrs. Graydon was a Presbyterian, she threw herself wholeheartedly into a fund-raising project to restore the Methodists' Cokesbury. Much of the proceeds from her cookbook went to help in the restoration. She attended a Methodist Conference in Charleston to request their support in the project and initiated the effort to display the world-famous Dali Jewel collection to raise money. A scrapbook of the restoration won a state award in the 1960s.

She also raised funds to buy fifty acres of land at Cokesbury to be used as a Youth Center and was instrumental in securing the 1840 house of Dr. Thomas Gary in Cokesbury. The home has been leased to the Ridge District of the State Division of the United Daughters of the Confederacy. It is used for local and district chapter meetings.

Endowed with boundless energy and enthusiasm, Mrs. Graydon was generous with her time and money, whether the cause was "Save a Puppy" or "Aid in World Relief."

During World War II she worked as a volunteer Red Cross nurse's aid. She served on the Cokesbury College Board of Trustees and was elected chairman of the Cokesbury Historical and Recreational Commission of Greenwood County.

The people of Greenwood and South Carolina showed their appreciation with numerous awards: the South Carolina Electric and Gas Company's preservation trophy given by the South Carolina Federation of Women's Clubs for outstanding achievements promoting South Carolina history, a life membership in the Garden Club of South Carolina, the honor award of the Greenwood Chapter of the American Association of University Women, Greenwood's Historical Award of Distinction from the Historical Society, and the Greenwood Rotary Club Service Community Award. Lander College awarded her a doctorate degree.

For her achievements she is listed in *Who's Who of American Women* and the *Dictionary of International Biography.*

Mrs. Graydon was a member of the Daughters of the American Revolution and the United Daughters of the Confederacy.

In her latter years she enjoyed a very special relationship with her great-grandchildren. Mrs. Graydon died on July 14, 1986—twelve years after the death of her husband. She is buried in Edgewood Cemetery in Greenwood.

With her enthusiastic love of the past, Mrs. Nell Saunders Graydon contributed to the present and the future by endowing lovers of history and of South

Carolina with a rich legacy. Her work of preservation and of capturing the grandeur, romance, and beauty of the past will continue to enrich the lives of people of all ages.

Josephine Pinckney

AUTHOR
1895–1957

Josephine forgot the fricasseed chicken on her plate. Instead, she let her glance flick back and forth across the long dinner table from aunt to uncle to cousin. She didn't want to miss any hint of a clash of personalities. That always livened up these drawn-out family get-togethers. A pang of guilt cast a shadow against the excitement stirring within her over the expectation of a quarrel. She leaned forward and looked down the row of dining chairs toward her mother. Did she remember their conversation earlier in the day?

"Well," Josephine had complained, "I don't want to go to grandmother's and be bored by Cousin So-and-So who always feels sorry for himself or that old disagreeable Aunt Thingummy who has a beard."

"Now, Josephine," her mother had frowned in reply, "you don't know how fortunate you are to have family around you. And anyway, you have to learn in life to get along with people you don't like."

Secretly though, Josephine enjoyed these family affairs, and now she felt bad about worrying her mother over not wanting to go.

Looking back, Josephine considered herself lucky to have come along in the heyday of the vanishing institution of visiting "relations." Brought up as an only child, since her older half brother lived with his mother's people in Virginia, Josephine liked the friction that was bound to surface when so many "kin" congregated.

"As I remember it," she recalled, "we were quite disagreeable to a clutch of cousins whom nobody liked but who had to be asked because they were kin. But they didn't seem to mind as they always turned up—either because they couldn't be insulted or else they came for the food."

In the course of those years Josephine remained endlessly fascinated by the mysterious kinship that links people to others of their blood, no matter how much they bicker. For, she felt, it is this entanglement that makes drama of the commonplace of family relationships. Often, she observed, new elements come in—through marriage mostly—and this brings something really startling.

It was on such events that Josephine based most of her writing. *Three O'Clock Dinner* tells of two contrasting families—one the aristocratic Redcliffs of Charleston and the other the immigrant Hessenwinkles—thrown together in marriage. A Literary Guild selection in 1945, the novel sold over 700,000 copies in America alone and made Miss Pinckney famous. The book received the Southern Authors Award for "the most distinguished book about the South by a Southerner." It was said she captured the life of Charleston as she knew it with all its pride, pettiness, and jaunty courage and preserved it in her writing.

"I did not take these characters from my own kith and kin," she said. "It's more fun to imagine people than to copy them from a family album. Besides," she added with a hint of mirth, "I want to live, and I would prefer to go on living in Charleston."

Mrs. Pinckney's writing was not only influenced by her family but also inspired by the Low Country with its cypress swamps, fluting calls of birds over tidal marshes, and great sea turtles crawling up beaches at midnight to lay their eggs. She painted word pictures of this spectral beauty in a 1927 volume of poetry titled *Sea-Drinking Cities*. Voted the best book of verse published by a Southerner, it received the Caroline Sinkler Prize. This early discipline of writing poetry, it was said, helped in developing the "chiseled" style of her prose.

At a time when poverty was commonplace, Josephine Lyons Scott Pinckney was born in affluence on January 25, 1895. Both of Josephine's parents inherited wealth; her mother, Camella Scott, was from an old Richmond family. The Pinckney dwelling on 29 Legare had its gable end to the street in typical Charleston "single house" fashion and was entered through a downstairs piazza.

Josephine was the descendant of Colonel Charles and Eliza Lucas Pinckney. The Pinckney family distinguished itself in state government with two governors and with framers of the Constitution, as well as through many other contributions.

Later the Pinckneys moved to a four-story mansion with an elevator on 21 King Street. They also owned a 450-acre plantation, El Dorado, on the Santee River. Mr. Pinckney was one of the last rice planters.

Josephine was the first student to enroll in Ashley Hall, where she was active in dramatics. With a love for literature, she always kept her blue copybook in good use. When she and her friends put out *Cerberus*, the literary magazine still published today, Josephine drew the lots for writing the poetry and jokes. Later she studied English at the College of Charleston, Radcliffe, and Boston University. In 1934 William and Mary College awarded her an honorary Phi Beta Kappa.

Although Miss Pinckney published poems nationally from 1921–35, she abandoned poetry for prose with the publishing of *Hilton Head* in 1940. The book tells of Henry Woodward, a young English surgeon who was the first English settler of South Carolina and who served as a middleman between Indians and whites. Set in 1663, the novel is not just a historical narrative but a psychological portrayal of the character's inner struggle.

It was from her childhood nurse who sang spirituals in the kitchen that Josephine gathered memories to write *The Great Mischief,* published in 1948.

She had listened with shivering delight to her nurse's Gullah tales of hags, witches, ghosts, devils, dried blood of bats, and a magic ball stuffed with lizards' legs. Though Timothy Partridge, the main character of the novel, dabbles in old tomes and witches' brew, he is actually on a search for the meaning of good and evil. *The Great Mischief* became a Book-of-the Month Club selection.

Other published works include *My Son and Foe,* with a Caribbean setting, in 1952 and *Splendid in Ashes,* a social comedy of Charleston, published posthumously in 1958.

South Caroliniana Library

With her sophisticated, confident air, the trim and precise Miss Pinckney was ahead of the times in her thinking. Such writers as James Joyce, William Faulkner, and Karl Marx prompted many of her ideas. One critic spoke of her as the "first literary citizen of South Carolina."

Most of her writing was accomplished at 36 Chalmers Street, a house she shared with her black cocker spaniel. In 1910 she bought and restored the faded lavender stucco house with its purple morning glories trailing on the wrought-iron fence. From her third-floor study she could view Washington Park.

Typical of her upbringing, Miss Pinckney was an expert hostess, entertaining such legendary figures as George Gershwin, Henry Mencken, Clare Boothe Luce, and Wendell Wilkie.

Her hobbies included collecting china and first-edition books, as well as gardening. She also collected and transcribed spirituals, which she sang with a group called the Society for the Preservation of Spirituals.

Always cultural minded, Miss Pinckney served as a trustee of the Charleston Museum, and as a member of the Historic Charleston Foundation she was active in the restoration of the Dock Street Theatre, one of the earliest centers of drama in America. Along with DuBose Heyward, Hervey Allen, and John Bennett, she started the Poetry Society of South Carolina in 1920. This same group formed the Charleston Renaissance. She was also a member of the Carolina Art Association.

During World War II Josephine served as a Civil Defense volunteer and assisted the home service department of the Red Cross.

Sometimes described as a cosmopolitan Charlestonian, she traveled abroad, spending a year in Italy. Often she wintered in New York and Provincetown, a small music and arts colony outside Boston. Occasionally she summered in Mexico. Yet she always returned to her home and garden in Charleston, just as her family had for generations.

On October 4, 1957, Josephine died of a respiratory infection. She was in New York completing revisions on *Splendid in Ashes*. She was sixty-two. Burial took place in Magnolia Cemetery.

Josephine Pinckney's life was marked not only by high achievement in letters but by a deep love for her city and its people. A citation was awarded posthumously by the America Scenic and Historic Preservation Society for her deep and fruitful interest in architectural preservation. Her remaining wealth benefited Charleston libraries, art, and other cultural groups. Ten thousand dollars went to the Medical Society of South Carolina for the establishment of a free dental clinic. Early family possessions were left to the Charleston Museum. In 1988 Miss Pinckney was inducted into the South Carolina Academy of Authors' Hall of Fame.

In recent years the Chalmers Street home of this literary artist and independent woman of the twentieth century has been included in the spring tour of the Historical Charleston Foundation.

Septima Poinsette Clark

EDUCATOR, CIVIL RIGHTS CRUSADER
1898–1987

On September 9, 1916, eighteen-year-old Septima Poinsette stood with her mother and a friend on the Tradd Street wharf in Charleston, South Carolina. She was leaving her family for the first time. Just off shore a gasoline launch shifted in the moving water—waiting to take her to her first teaching assignment on Johns Island.

Although Septima had grown up in Charleston, she had little knowledge about the many sea islands along the coast. For all she knew, she could be headed toward some strange land across the Atlantic.

Great waves of longing stirred within her as the launch pushed along wide rivers and intracoastal waterways. Homesickness overshadowed her lifelong dream of becoming a teacher.

The launch, with its few passengers, wound through creeks and marshy channels. Once it was necessary to drop anchor and wait for the tide to cover the mud flats. The journey, which should have taken an hour, took almost nine hours.

Septima's arrival at the Promise Land School on Johns Island did not help to raise her spirits. The black, creosote-coated building held benches without backs, an ax for getting firewood, and a bucket and dipper for drinking water. Teaching materials were sorely inadequate.

Attendance was poor. Some of the students walked eight or ten miles to school. During harvest season, the older students did not come at all, except on rainy days. Even then, if the sun came out, a plantation wagon pulled up to get their tenants' children to work on the farm.

Living conditions on the island matched the school in crudeness. Newspapers lined the inside of the houses for warmth. Lanterns, hanging on nails from rafters, served as lighting. The attic where Septima and a fellow teacher stayed had no heat except the chimney running through it. During winter Septima suffered frostbite from her long walks to school in the freezing weather.

In spite of the adverse conditions, Septima came to love the people on the island. Such caring, she believed, came from her father, who was born into slavery. As a boy on the Poinsett Plantation, he had the task of carrying the books of his master's son. Both boys rode the same horse to the schoolhouse, but Septima's father grazed the animal outside until school was out. Peter Porcher Poinsette was an old man before he learned to write his name. Yet his heart held no animosity—only an inborn love for all people. He struggled to see that his own children had the opportunity to learn, and when his daughter Septima became a teacher, he was proud she was going into such an honorable profession.

Fortunately Septima had no difficulty understanding the Gullah dialect of the island. Many of the people on Henrietta Street where she grew up spoke the same way.

One thing that did bother her, though, was that just across the street from her two-teacher school with 132 pupils was a white school with fewer than half that many students. Those teachers were paid $85 a month. Septima and the other black teacher received $35.

Regardless of the frustrations involved, Septima joined with the people of the island in their gatherings: parties at the end of harvesting, celebrations when sugar cane was made into syrup, and even all-night wakes when someone died.

She had come a long way, and for that Septima was grateful to her parents. Like her father, Septima's mother had dreams for their eight children. Born a "free issue" in Haiti, she received an education from books. To support the family, Septima's parents worked at many jobs: her mother taking in washing and ironing, her father catering parties and working as a janitor.

One of Septima's earliest memories is of her father walking her to school when she was five. Her old black teacher had great pride and demanded that her students have it too. A strict disciplinarian, she did not allow chewing gum or laughing at something taking place in school. A misspelled word brought a whipping in the hand for each letter missed.

After the private black school, Septima attended Mary Street School, a public school for blacks. A timid child, she was afraid of everybody and everything. One day a visitor brought canaries to show her class. Miss Seabrook, her white teacher, had the students write stories about the visit. She praised Septima's paper, and from then on Septima felt better.

As a ninth grader Septima attended Avery Normal Institute, begun in the 1890s by the American Missionary Association. Most of the teachers came from the New England states.

Septima loved school, yet she hated to be a burden on her family. She felt she should be working rather than continuing her schooling. An invitation to be a housemaid for a young black couple, a railway clerk and his wife, allowed her to do both. At graduation the Avery teachers urged Septima to go to college. Only by earning money could her dream of being a teacher come true; consequently, she took the teaching position at Johns Island and later at her alma mater, Avery.

Septima was serving on a USO social committee to entertain soldiers coming home from World War I when she met sailor Nerie David Clark from Hickory, North Carolina. In 1919 they were married.

It was also during her stay at Avery that she began to work for the cause of freedom and justice. She collected over twenty thousand signatures on a petition to have black teachers hired by the Charleston County School District. The law passed, and that year Septima taught in McClellanville, thirty-six miles from Charleston.

South Caroliniana Library

The loss of the couples' first baby and Nerie's being away in the Navy left Septima at loose ends. A stay with her husband's family in Hickory, North Carolina, allowed her to enroll at the Agricultural and Technical College in Greensboro for the 1922 session. The following fall she taught in a mountain school near Boone, North Carolina.

Upon her husband's discharge from service, the Clarks moved to Dayton, Ohio. Here they had a son, but happiness was short-lived: Nerie died at thirty-six with a kidney disorder.

Septima felt her only hope was to return to the schoolroom. She longed to return to the South Carolina Low Country with its rich smells and warm memories. Her affection for the people there led her back, and she found a sincere welcome, as well as improved conditions.

It was a source of pride to Septima that she could revert to the *patois* of the natives who had never left the island. She threw herself into helping combat illiteracy and teaching the women to sew. It was her work on the island that set Septima on a course of helping the underprivileged. For in helping these people raise themselves to a better status in life, she felt she was serving her state and nation.

For the sake of a better environment for her son, Septima left Johns Island after three years for Columbia. Here she was able to participate in civic activities. She helped raise money for many special programs, especially a home in Cayce for underprivileged girls.

Although segregated by race, she and other blacks were allowed to attend lectures in institutions in Columbia other than the Negro colleges, Allen and Benedict. Septima counted this a privilege.

In Charleston Septima had worked to change the law so that black teachers could teach in public schools. Now through the National Association for the Advancement of Colored People she worked to make black teachers' salaries equal to whites' with comparable certificates. As a result, South Carolina teachers were required to take a national teachers' examination. Septima took the test and made an A.

After studying during summers at Columbia University in New York, at Atlanta University, and taking extension courses, Septima earned a bachelor of arts degree from Benedict College in 1942. In three more summers at Hampton Institute in Virginia, she earned a master's degree.

During these busy years, Septima's son, Nerie, Jr., spent much of his time with his Clark grandparents in Hickory.

In 1949, after eighteen years of teaching in Columbia public schools, as well as in an adult night program directed by Miss Wil Lou Gray, Septima returned to Charleston. Her father had died, and her mother needed her.

In Charleston she renewed her work with the Tuberculosis Association and the Young Women's Christian Association and aided in the organization of similar groups for young men. She also worked with the Metropolitan Council of Negro Women and black sororities to provide college scholarships for deserving girls.

Her friendship with Judge and Mrs. J.W. Waring supported her work for equality among the races. For this friendship, Septima and the Warings suffered open criticism from both races.

Of all the organizations in which she participated, Septima felt the NAACP the most rewarding. In 1954 the U.S. Supreme Court handed down the opinion that segregation of public schools was unconstitutional. The deciding case originated in South Carolina.

Because of her affiliation with the NAACP and the United Council of Church Women, as well as her invitation to an integrationist to speak at a PTA meeting, Septima lost her job: her teaching contract was canceled. She also lost her teachers' retirement benefits after thirty years in the profession. Such action from the state she loved caused much heartache.

Perhaps Septima's most significant achievement came as a result of this termination. She began establishing Citizenship Schools throughout the South. Remembering the pitiful illiteracy on Johns Island, where some people could not even use a calendar to mark the births of their children, she began—with the help of volunteers—her work on the sea islands. Bernice Robinson became the first volunteer teacher.

Septima modeled her schools on the Chattanooga, Tennessee, Highlander Folk School. Highlander had been organized in 1932 by Dr. Lilian Johnson, a white woman from Memphis, to help poor mountain people who were culturally and emotionally starved.

When Septima further developed her idea at the Highlander Folk School, run by a white Southerner, Miles Horton, authorities seemed determined to end Septima's activities here too. On a fabricated charge of possession of liquor, authorities raided the school and arrested Septima and three young men. Their pictures and the charges made the front page of the newspapers.

Septima was determined not to be bitter. It was said she could lecture on the ills and injustices of racial segregation and never let her voice rise above a whisper. She maintained that nonviolent dignity now.

After the closing of the Highlander School, she continued to work to educate black adults and to help them understand the basic structure of the government. She did this under the sponsorship of the Southern Christian Leadership Conference headed by Dr. Martin Luther King, Jr.

Septima admitted that her faith sometimes wore thin during her struggles. She never failed to acknowledge that mistakes had been made, but always—she believed—they were errors of judgment rather than motive.

She was, however, granted her state retirement benefits eventually, and she was elected to the Charleston County School Board, which had earlier failed to renew her contract.

Many honors came to Mrs. Clark for her pioneer efforts for civil rights. In 1978 the College of Charleston awarded her an honorary doctorate—the first black the college had so honored. In 1979 she was among seventeen "aged" black Americans honored at the White House by President Carter. In 1982 she received the Order of the Palmetto, the highest award South Carolina can present to its civilians, and in 1985, the Wil Lou Gray Award from the South Carolina Gerontological Society.

Mrs. Clark was twice honored by the SCLC. An expressway in Charleston and a day care center she founded after unattended children died in a fire are named for her.

Septima, whose name means "sufficient," lived out her years at the home she loved on 17 Henrietta Street. The white-framed, typical Charleston home harbored memories of her childhood and the parents who inspired her love of learning.

This legendary educator and humanitarian died at the age of eighty-nine. She is buried in the Old Bethel Cemetery in Charleston.

Modjeska Montieth Simkins

CIVIL RIGHTS PIONEER
1899–1992

The crack of a gunshot woke Modjeska, her mother, and her younger sister to the dimness of the early morning hours. The threat to Modjeska's father had come true: someone had fired into the Simkins' home.

"Throw a quilt on the floor and get on it." Her father, in his fearless way, thought only of his family as he readied to return the fire.

Henry Clarence Montieth was working in Eldorado, Arkansas, as the foreman of a brickwork project when a mob tried to run him out of town. The sudden

South Caroliniana Library

death of a white supervisor had left Montieth in charge. White hod-carriers revolted against working under a black man. Fortunately for the intruders, Montieth had reached for his shotgun rather than his Winchester rifle. Only one of the night mobsters suffered a wound.

For the remainder of the project—the building of a jail—two gunmen kept Modjeska's father under protection. Fearful for his family, Montieth sent his wife and two children ahead to his next work place, Converse, South Carolina. Thus, Modjeska learned early about man's inhumanity to man.

Modjeska, the oldest of eight children, was born on December 5, 1899, on Pine Street in Columbia in the home her father had built for his bride, Rachel.

Because Modjeska's father did not want his daughters to grow up to work in menial jobs, he later moved his family to a farm on the outskirts of Columbia. There he and Rachel endeavored to teach their children the value of a penny. They also instilled in them that "No one is any better than you are unless he behaves better than you."

Modjeska's mother, a former teacher, always read to the children. Modjeska particularly remembers *Girl of the Limberlost, Pilgrim's Progress,* and Bible stories. The love of reading became so much a part of her life that Modjeska says, "Even now I never go to sleep until I have read something to enrich my life."

She also remembers following her mother down country paths as she walked to help others. Always a caring person, Rachel Montieth organized the Second Calvary Church in her home.

In 1908 Modjeska started first grade on the Benedict campus. There she was taught by northerners who had come south as missionaries to educate the freed Negroes. These dedicated teachers saw to it that Modjeska and the others received a classical education in literature and the languages.

After graduation from Benedict College, Modjeska taught mathematics at Booker T. Washington High School.

In 1929 she married Andrew Whitfield Simkins, a businessman from Edgefield. Andrew's father had been a slave. With the marriage Modjeska became a mother to his five children, all under fifteen years of age.

Since married women were not allowed to teach, Modjeska began working for the South Carolina Tuberculosis Association, where she labored to instruct others about basic health and sanitation.

When Modjeska was fifty-five, she began working for the Victory Savings Bank in Columbia. After serving as supervisor for the bookkeeping department, she became a branch manager and a member of the Board of Trustees.

Always sensitive to the needs of her people, Modjeska worked as a volunteer in the NAACP. In 1940 she became co-founder and secretary of the South Carolina Conference of this group. She was instrumental in helping to establish other NAACP chapters around the state. She also became a staff member of the Associated Negro Press, which gave her a voice to oppose injustices toward blacks.

Against this background she worked toward integrating schools, improving jobs, opening political participation, and obtaining decent housing. Basically, Modjeska sought to promote social and economic justice for all. "All people," she said, "want the right to work, to live, to properly educate their children, to enjoy protection of its government, and to be citizens in a world that belongs to no one group."

As she worked toward that goal, Modjeska became friends with some of the nation's fighters for civil rights. Among them were Justice Thurgood Marshall, Dr. Benjamin Mays, Mary McCleod Bethune, Dr. W.E.B. Du Bois, and singer Paul Robeson.

Often unpopular in her state for challenging politicians and others to "do something about deplorable conditions," Modjeska sees herself as one who works for pride and self-respect for all the world's underprivileged.

Honors for her efforts toward these goals have come in many forms. In 1966 she was appointed to the Richland County Economic Opportunity Commission. A Modjeska Simkins Fund honors her for her pioneering work to extend the rights of freedom of speech and association of the workplace. This award is given annually to an individual or an organization whose leadership has significantly contributed to human dignity and whose work has forged new solutions to community problems.

Modjeska's husband died in 1965. From her Columbia home on 2025 Mario Street, Modjeska Simkins' spirit remained undaunted in her fight for Americans' basic rights. She died on April 5, 1992, at the age of ninety-two. She is buried in Palmetto Cemetery.

Lucile Ellerbe Godbold

OLYMPIC MEDALIST
1900–1981

A tall sinewy woman stepped into the circle to prepare for the shot-put event. For a moment fear seized her. Then the familiar voice of Dr. Stewart, her United States coach, rang out: "Now show 'em what South Carolina can do."

Lucile Godbold did just that. Her throw was twenty-two meters (just over seventy-two feet), establishing a new world's record. The crowd in the Olympic Stadium roared. Cameras clicked.

The year was 1922 in Paris. Lucile had just graduated from Winthrop College when she won six medals as a part of the U.S. Olympic team. No other South Carolinian, man or woman, had ever accomplished this feat. It was also the first year that international Olympics were open to women. Lucile won first-place gold medals in the shot-put and the hop-step-jump and finished second in the basketball throw for distance. She placed third in the javelin and the

1,000-meter race and fourth in the 300-meter race. In all, she won an amazing eighteen points.

When Lucile returned from the games, her hometown of Estill honored her with a parade. She was also honored by her alma mater. Dr. D.B. Johnson, president of Winthrop, who had gone abroad to see his school's representative perform, told the Winthrop student body, "Every leading newspaper in every

Winthrop College

Lucile Godbold practicing for the Olympics

civilized country in the world has made mention of her."

"Miss Ludy," as her friends and students knew her, recalled modestly, "Athletes of today would not think these distances very far. More emphasis is placed on sports today, and athletes begin training earlier. They also benefit from better methods of training."

Miss Ludy was born in Marion, South Carolina, on May 31, 1900, and attended schools in McColl and Wagener, "I can't remember," she said, "when I was not interested in sports. And in college I was determined to be among the best in athletics."

The annual track meet at Winthrop was the beginning. There she broke three American records: shot-put, discus, and hop-step-jump.

Lucile's determination paid off, for preparation for the Olympian competition took many long and hard hours of practice. Often Lucile would be the only person on Winthrop's athletic field, but her will to succeed led her on.

In Mamaroneck, New York, she readily won a place among the United States' representatives to Paris. Knowing her determination and her skill, Winthrop girls helped her raise the funds.

That same year, 1922, Lucile Godbold became director of physical education at Columbia College, Columbia, South Carolina. There her friendly good humor, despite her fierce bellows on the hockey field, made her an unforgettable personality.

During summers Miss Ludy and her sister Sarah—also a physical education teacher—ran Camp Jocassee in the South Carolina foothills.

In the "Faculty Foolies," performed at Columbia College, she often brought the house down. Dressed in a red flapper's dress with high-heeled shoes and a long cigarette holder, she performed as "Flaming Mame."

In 1961 Miss Ludy was the first woman to be named in the South Carolina Athletic Hall of Fame. She was selected for *Who's Who in American Sports, Who's Who of American Women, Outstanding Personalities of the South, Dictionary of International Biography,* and *World Who's Who of Women in Education.*

Columbia College honored Miss Ludy by dedicating the 1950 yearbook to her and more recently by proclaiming "Ludy Day" and naming the new physical educational building Godbold Center. Annually, a "Ludy Bowl," a powder-puff football game, is played by the Columbia College girls.

In 1972, to commemorate the fiftieth anniversary of Miss Ludy's accomplishments, Estill erected a marker by the town hall in her honor. It reads:

Lucile Ellerbe Godbold

1922 Gold Medal winner [in] Paris, France, while a student at Winthrop College. First woman in South Carolina Athletic Hall of Fame. Outstanding educator at Columbia College. Daughter of William Asa and Lucile Ellerbe Godbold, Estill, South Carolina. Formerly of Marion, South Carolina. Miss Ludy was born May 31, 1900, at the Godbold place, Marion County.

When Miss Ludy saw the marker, she replied with her usual humor, "My gosh, they've already written my epitaph."

In 1980, after teaching physical education at Columbia College for fifty-eight years, Miss Ludy retired. She died April 7, 1981, and is buried at the Lawtonville Cemetery in Estill, South Carolina.

Annie Greene Nelson

FIRST BLACK WOMAN OF LETTERS
1902–1993

"All right, hurry up now. It's gonna be daylight soon and we gotta get all our things to the Parrot Plantation before dey miss us."

Annie couldn't see her daddy's face and thick red hair in the dimness, but she knew he was still fiery mad and she didn't blame him. With all her nine-year-old strength she helped load their personal belongings from the two-room house onto the wagon, which she could barely see in the dim light. Then she hustled back inside to help with the other children.

The overseer of the place where they lived had said her mamma had to be back in the field the next day, but her daddy had told him Mamma needed more time after the birth of the baby. And her daddy was right. The only way they could stay, the man said, was if her mamma worked the next day. That left Annie's daddy no choice but to slip away in the night. Otherwise, he wouldn't be allowed to take his cow and the chickens and other possessions that rightfully belonged to him.

Fleeing in the dead of night from a cruel landowner in Darlington County made such an impression on young Annie that many years later she wrote the play "Parrott's Plantation." Though based on a tragic happening, Annie was able to incorporate humor in this story of black sharecropping experience in 1910. The play was performed in Columbia and by the workshop theater of Brooklyn College in New York.

The oldest of thirteen children, Annie Greene was born in the Cartersville area of Darlington County on December 5, 1902, to Nancy Muldrow and Sylvester Greene. Annie remembers her mother as proud and strict. "If she promised a switching before the sun went down," Annie recalls, "there was no changing her."

The memory of her father's love for his children is an important part of her life. He taught Annie to read at a young age, and the love for reading and writing has never left her. Loving and forgiving, he stood his ground on one thing—his oldest daughter shouldn't have much to do with boys.

"He was the kindest man in the world," Annie said of her father. "He walked seven or eight miles on Sunday to teach a Sunday School class, and he taught singing in our home. He did love to sing."

The household regularly reserved a time of prayer and Bible reading; thus, Annie has always considered Christianity the foundation of her existence. Annie says, "My father's prayers and encouragement followed me through. He always said, 'Grow up thinking what you are going to be.' "

Annie's childhood was a busy one. At eight years of age she fixed breakfast for the family and milked cows. The seven-mile walk to school was a long one, but Annie's mother folded newspapers and slipped them between their under-clothing to ward off colds in their chests. In season she worked in the fields. Her parents could not stay home with the children, so the children picked cotton too—the small ones with their little flour sacks for cotton bags.

After graduating from Darlington County Schools, Annie attended Benedict College and Voorhees, where she earned a degree in education and nursing. She worked as a nurse and as a school teacher in Darlington, Lexington, and Richland counties. At one time she served as a supervisor of 4-H clubs and taught adult education. She also founded and taught in the first kindergarten for black children in Columbia.

Marriage to Edward Nelson on June 10, 1935, brought Annie to Columbia. The couple had eleven children, six of whom are still living. Mrs. Nelson had twenty-three grandchildren and six great-grandchildren. She lost her husband in 1979.

Throughout her life Mrs. Nelson remembered incidents from her childhood. She had heard that her great-grandmother was kidnapped as a child and sold into slavery. Her grandparents, Claiborne and Mary Berry, were slaves. Annie heard half-whispers telling of lynching, murder, and cruelty. She remembers, too, the terrible accident when her baby brother burned to death in front of her eyes. But she also remembers the happy times, especially on the Parrotts' plantation. She thinks of her father singing and praying in the field.

Because of all she had witnessed among her people, Annie felt she must put into words the deprivation, fears, joys, and abiding courage of her race.

Her lifelong love of reading and her father's gift for telling tales—which she often heard at night by listening secretly to the adults talking—made storytelling come naturally for her.

In 1942, while keeping house and caring for her children, Mrs. Nelson wrote *After the Storm*. With the publication of that work by Hampton Publishing Company, Annie Greene Nelson became the first black woman in South Carolina to write and publish a novel.

The Dawn Appears followed in 1944 and *Don't Walk on My Dreams* in 1961. *Shadows of the South Land* was serialized in *the Palmetto Leader*, a black newspaper, in 1952. She also wrote a musical drama about an unemployed teacher during the Depression. It was presented at Benedict College.

In her books Mrs. Nelson captured an era that might otherwise be lost. Using real people and places under the guise of different names, she tells of Maw, who would throw an old shoe at Paw for luck before he went fishing or throw

Maxie Roberts

salt in the fire to stop an owl from hollering.

There was Sugar Babe who wanted to be a teacher so badly that she even tried to walk prim and proper like her teacher, Miss Henrietta. She practiced walking like her up and down the cotton rows. And there were parents who worked in white people's houses and brought that culture home to their children.

Thus, Mrs. Nelson captures people who lived plain and simple lives with childlike faith in God.

Granny Jenny in *Don't Walk on My Dreams* embarrassed the daughter who brought her to New York by singing, even on the streets. "I got something inside dat sings," she said. "My soul dats happy." All the family back South on the plantation were her "chillin," and she wanted to go home. The family welcomed her back. They loved her and would "see after her 'til she crossed over."

Mrs. Nelson writes of the special bonds between the whites and blacks of the South, of some fine black people and some that "want a bitta good," of a white gin owner who wouldn't take anything "off no 'biggety nigger.'"

Much of her love of writing Mrs. Nelson attributes to her close friendship with Everette Love Blair, Jesse Stuart's biographer.

Other than being a writer, Mrs. Nelson is also a performer. During World War II she and three of her children performed in *The Missing Link*, one of her plays. She is a popular speaker in schools and colleges.

In 1980 Mrs. Nelson received the Columbia Community Drama Award and an arts award from the Columbia Urban League. She was also awarded the J. Scott Kennedy Award for dedication to black theater. In 1989 she received the Lucy Bostick Award from the Friends of Richmond County Library. She is included in the Afro-American Novel Project of the University of Mississippi. Benedict College paid tribute to Mrs. Annie Greene Nelson in 1989 during Black History Month.

The little girl from the plantation fields who faced obstacles in realizing her dreams danced in a castle in Quebec and traveled with her grandchildren to Algeria. The first South Carolina "black woman of letters" died December 22, 1993.

Gwen Bristow

HISTORICAL NOVELIST
1903–1980

Gwen dropped her last quarter in the newspaper stand and took out another copy of *The Record,* Columbia's evening newspaper. At the age of twelve she had a piece on the "School Page" about field day competitions at her school. Her name was printed at the end of the article. *She was now the writer she always dreamed she would be.*

Gwen Bristow was born on September 16, 1903, in Marion, South Carolina, where she spent her early years. Later, her minister father, Louis Judson, moved his family to Abbeville.

In high school Gwen worked on the school's newspaper. During her senior year she wrote a two-act play, which was presented at graduation. She also gave the salutatory address, an original composition that was published in the high school's *Proper Gander* by the class of 1920.

Excited over the staging of her play, Gwen continued to write drama. Several of her plays were performed in the colleges she attended—Anderson and Judson. After receiving a bachelor of arts degree from Judson, she went on to study journalism at Columbia University in New York.

Since her father was a clergyman, there was little money in the family, but Gwen managed to find ways to help out with her schooling: she worked as a nursemaid for children of the wealthy, typed theses for graduate students, and wrote rags-to-riches biographies of successful businessmen to sell to trade journals. She was also a secretary to a European baroness who had come to the United States after World War I.

From the school of journalism, Gwen went to New Orleans to work on the *Times-Picayune*. There she covered holdups, murders, meetings of Rotary Clubs, football games, and investigations of Huey Long. She spent many long hours waiting for juries to make up their minds and nearly got shot during a jailbreak. She interviewed celebrities and political candidates, wrote Sunday feature articles about romantic spots, went out on still-smashing expeditions with the Prohibition raiders, rode an elephant in the circus, and covered the Mississippi River flood.

It was while she was a reporter in New Orleans that Gwen met another reporter, Bruce Manning. Bruce had been advised by his doctor to seek a milder climate. When he arrived in New Orleans, the city was in the grips of a cold snap.

"Lady," he said to the girl reporter standing beside him, "where does the South begin?"

Although Gwen's paper, the *Times-Picayune,* was the rival of Bruce's paper, the *Item,* the two got along well together. They were married a year later.

Both reporters loved to do their own private scribbling in off hours from their jobs. Unfortunately, the cheap apartment where they lived had the constant blare of a radio from next door at all hours. The couple tried everything they knew to put a stop to a disrupting situation. They asked nicely, threatened, and finally appealed to the police. Nothing worked.

The two devised various playful schemes whereby they might murder the inconsiderate man. While polishing up the best of their plans, they decided that the plot would make a good story—and they wrote it. The story line was worked into a book that became *The Invisible Host.* It was also made into a play, *The Ninth Guest,* and even into a movie.

The money they made from the book enabled them to move. Feeling quite proud of themselves, the couple quit their jobs and took a house on the Mississippi Gulf Coast. There they settled down to what they thought of as a literary life and collaborated on two more murder mysteries, published by Mystery League.

Unfortunately, the Depression came, and the former reporters found themselves back at their newspapers asking for their old jobs back. Bruce also began to write radio scripts, and Gwen kept writing novels while she covered current happenings for her editor.

In fact, Gwen worked very hard at writing fiction. The only problem was she couldn't find a publisher. After four unpublished novels, she was becoming unhappy with her writing life.

In 1934 Bruce had a chance to go to Hollywood and write screenplays, and so the couple moved to California.

At this time Gwen announced that she was giving up writing. Since Bruce wrote his screenplays at the Hollywood studio, they made no provisions for writing in their new home.

It wasn't long, however, before Gwen began to size up her situation. It had never before occurred to her to be anything but a writer. Yet there was absolutely no reason for her to continue writing *except* that it made her unhappy not to. "Even if nobody wants to read what I write," she told herself, "I still have to write."

So, almost stealthily—as if she might be caught—Gwen set up a card table in the corner of her bedroom and began novel number five.

This time she wrote about what she knew. She had lived in New Orleans for eight years and traveled every corner of the state. Thus, she began *Deep Summer,* the story of a family who might have lived in Louisiana in colonial times. After sending the manuscript off to a publisher, she soothed her patience by beginning a sequel. She called this manuscript *The Handsome Road.*

South Caroliniana Library

When the "blessed" letter of acceptance came from Thomas Crowell Company, she moved ahead with the final work in the trilogy, *This Side of Glory.* The three volumes took the aristocratic Larne family and the plebeian Upjohns from pre-Revolutionary days to the World War I. The three works of historical fiction, all published by Crowell, became *The Plantation Trilogy.*

While Bruce served overseas during World War II, Gwen wrote *Tomorrow Is Forever*. That book was made into a movie.

Jubilee Trail, published in 1950, tells of California days before the Gold Rush.

Gwen Bristow had realized her childhood dream—she was an author. Her mind constantly observed; ideas teased her thoughts. Too, she loved the research necessary to make readers feel they were really "there."

One day a friend who also loved books showed Gwen a beautifully bound edition of early American poetry. As Gwen turned the gilt-edged pages, her eyes fell on the verse:

> *Our band is few, but true and tried,*
> *Our leader frank and bold.*
> *The British soldier trembles*
> *When Marion's name is told.*

Suddenly Gwen was a little girl again in her South Carolina schoolroom. The teacher was reading "The Song of Marion's Men," by William Cullen Bryant, and telling the class about Francis Marion, the Carolina Swamp Fox of the American Revolution.

"Look out the window," her teacher was saying. "Once your playground lay splotched with the blood of men who fought and died so you could go to school. Don't ever forget what they did for you—those people of the Revolution, Marion's men and the women who stood behind them."

Gwen heard more about Marion from her mother, Caroline Cornelia, for her ancestor Nicholas Winkler had been one of Marion's men.

What, she wondered, were the people *really* like in the blackest days of the Revolution? But she didn't have to wonder long. She returned to Charleston to research a time when American money was worth two cents on the dollar and nobody could get a job unless he promised to be a good subject to King George III.

Thousands of hours of reading and studying allowed Gwen to immerse herself in the period: clothes, hairstyles, architecture, home furnishings, food, and travel. Maps showed her the areas Marion's men covered so she could recreate the time and place. Gwen even learned to weave in the Charleston Museum.

From this background came *Celia Garth*, the story of a girl from Charleston who was a spy for Marion's men. History comes alive as the king's whole army tries to catch the little man whom British General Tarleton called the Swamp Fox.

Gwen Bristow's books have been translated into many languages. *This Side of Glory* was chosen as a *Times Literary Supplement*.

She was a member of the Authors League of America, P.E.N., and Pen and Brush.

Gwen Bristow Manning, South Carolina author, died in California in 1980.

Hilla Sheriff

HEALTH PIONEER
1903–1988

Hilla leaned over the fluff of a "biddie" and concentrated for all she was worth on its little broken wing. Because she wanted to be a doctor when she grew up, she had charge of caring for the tiny chicks who became ill or got hurt in their frantic efforts to move in the same direction. In the small community near Easley in Pickens County, Hilla was known as the child who nursed the neighborhood animals back to health. Even in her solitary play with her paper dolls, she always took care to name one "The Doctor."

About the time Hilla was ready to begin public school, her parents, John Washington and Mary Lenora Smith Sheriff, moved their family of seven children to Orangeburg. There Mr. Sheriff went into the lumber business.

Throughout her schooling, Hilla never lost her dream of becoming a doctor. At first her family had looked upon her ambition as a childish fantasy. Even when she graduated from high school and entered the College of Charleston, a family member commented, "She'll be married before her first year is up."

Two years later, however, Hilla entered the Medical College of South Carolina in Charleston. She was one of three females in her class. Oddly enough, her worst fear was of the frogs they had to dissect. "I had a horror," she said, "that one of the cold things might jump on me." For her, the cadavers were far less frightening.

At the end of her sophomore year, Hilla was assigned to work in the eye clinic with Dr. Henry Zerbst. The ophthalmologist had been Hilla's instructor in an undergraduate course, and they had dated off and on. In fact, they had a date planned for the evening of the day she began her assignment with him.

Innocently Hilla asked the doctor how to spell *homatropine*. He looked down at her as if he had never seen her before in his life. "Young lady," he said, "if you want to know, look it up."

"I could have killed him," Hilla said later, "but I didn't want the nurses to know how embarrassed I was so I kept quiet."

For the remainder of her time in the clinic, she tried to get his attention to call off their date; but without being conspicuous, she wasn't able to do so.

Back at her boarding house, she asked her landlady to ring Henry's home and get him on the phone. (She didn't want his mother to know she was calling him.) "Or," she said, "just tell him the date's off."

"If I'm going to cancel the date," her landlady said, "at least I should know why."

When Hilla explained, the landlady said, "You silly little thing. He's the only one who comes around here who has any sense."

Still pursuing her goals, Hilla did a summer internship in Little Mountain Hospital in Alta Pass, North Carolina. After graduation she did another internship in Pennsylvania and a residency at Children's Hospital in Washington, D.C., as well as one at the Willard Parker Contagious Disease Hospital in New York City.

Answering sick calls in the crowded neighborhoods of the big cities awakened Hilla to the terrible aspects of poverty. Parents, who often spoke no English, did not understand when the strange people tried to take their children away to the hospital. Because death could come so quickly from diptheria, police often had to go on ambulance calls to "force" treatment for a child.

Even though opportunities came for Dr. Sheriff to practice elsewhere, she wanted to return to her native state. Thus, in 1929 she began her career in Spartanburg in pediatrics. During her four-year period as a pediatrician, she volunteered to conduct a clinic for the Health Department. The experience proved to be a turning point: helping the less fortunate through a public health program fulfilled her lifelong dream.

Sadly, Dr. Sheriff was faced with thousands of cases of pellagra in Spartanburg County. She knew the disease could be prevented by adding vitamins to the diet, yet even if drugstore vitamins were available, few patients could have afforded them. Worse still, the afflicted knew nothing of the value of leafy green vegetables. The South planted cotton, not vegetables.

Dr. Sheriff knew that more financial help was needed than the county could provide. Under her direction, relief came from the American Women's Hospital Service. The humanitarian relief, begun in Europe after World War I, now answered its first call in the United States in Spartanburg County.

In 1931 Dr. Sheriff, a nutritionist, and a nurse began to operate a healthmobile—a kind of wagon hitched to a Model A Ford—about the Spartanburg countryside. Conducting a campaign against pellagra and other preventable diseases, they organized thirty-one health centers, where they held clinics to teach people to eat the right foods. In the healthmobile they actually prepared foods like oatmeal and raisins in a attempt to get the undernourished to eat foods with nutritional value.

They immunized children against diptheria and whooping cough and examined pregnant women. They worked toward educating people about sanitary conditions to prevent typhoid fever.

The team enlisted mill executives to set up "health houses" near their plants. In "Little Mother's Classes," they taught eight and nine year olds about personal hygiene and caring for the babies at home while the mothers worked in the mill.

In 1936 Dr. Sheriff was one of four persons in the United States to win a Rockefeller Foundation Scholarship for post-graduate studies in public health at Harvard. Upon her return to Spartanburg, she served on the medical and teaching staffs of Spartanburg General Hospital.

Under the direction of Dr. Sheriff, Spartanburg County Health Department saw the development of the nation's first family clinic sponsored by a county health department. Mothers, encouraged to bring their children to the clinic, funded through the Millbank Memorial Fund of New York City, found a caring, compassionate friend in Dr. Sheriff. A child sitting on her lap was a common sight.

Dr. Sheriff's most pressing concern became the mothers—many in their thirties, tired and unhealthy, were expecting their fifteenth or twentieth child. Often these mothers died, leaving all those children behind. In 1940 South

South Caroliniana Library

Carolina became the first state to have family planning in its health department.

The year 1940 was important to Dr. Sheriff for another reason: she married Dr. Henry Zerbst, the Charleston ophthalmologist, whom she had dated off and on for eighteen years. He insisted that Hilla keep her maiden name to avoid confusion about which doctor was wanted on the phone. Also, he said she had worked hard in her profession and should retain her own name.

Both doctors had an appreciation for the other's career. When asked why they hadn't married earlier, Dr. Sheriff always answered with a gentle hint of amusement, "It was hard to find courting time."

George enjoyed gourmet cooking, and when the couple could arrange to do so, they spent the afternoon target shooting as recreation. Unfortunately, after thirteen years of marriage, George died.

In her position as Director of Maternal and Child Health, Dr. Sheriff continued to pioneer programs against child abuse and neglect. She worked for better care for premature babies and for a test to detect mental retardation early so a special diet could be given to those children. She also formed clinics to further the education of granny midwives to provide better care for mothers in home deliveries.

In 1968 Dr. Sheriff organized thirteen health districts throughout the state and remained responsible for their administration. She did not stop at county or even state boundaries: she spoke at international medical conferences and served as a delegate to Australia for the International Women's Medical Conference.

Dr. Sheriff was a representative to the White House Conferences on Children and Youth over three decades. The state Board of Health's *Monthly Bulletin,* as well as many professional journals, carried articles expressing her views on the health needs of families. She served in more than twenty associations—often as president or vice-president—and on countless boards.

In recognition of her services, she is listed in *Who's Who in America, American Women, South and Southwest, Health Care, Two Thousand Women of Achievement,* and *Personalities of the South.*

Upon her retirement after a forty-five-year career, Dr. Sheriff was the deputy commissioner of the state Department of Health and Environmental Control and chief of the Bureau of Community Health Services.

She received the first Ross Award for outstanding service in the maternal and child health field in the Southeast in 1969, the Meritorious Award of South Carolina Mental Health Association in 1972, the J. Marion Sims Award and State Employee of the Year in 1974, the Order of the Palmetto in 1975, Distinguished Alumni Award of the Medical University of South Carolina in 1981, the William Weston Award in 1983, and the South Carolina American Academy of Pediatrics Achievement Award and South Carolina Hospital Association's Dedicated Service Award in 1986. A documentary film, *Carrying Health to the County,* depicted her career. The award she treasured most was one made for her by a mentally retarded child.

Always retaining the poise and manner of a lady, Dr. Sheriff lost her composure only when she spoke of suffering children. As one colleague said of her Southern femininity, "I think Scarlet O'Hara could take a few lessons from her."

Dr. Hilla Sheriff, health pioneer, died in 1988 and is buried in Greenlawn Memorial Park.

Nancy Jane Day

LIBRARIAN
1905–

A game of baseball with her brothers was the farthest thing from Nancy Jane's mind. The great red splotches of red measles confined her to bed and kept her from her first-grade class at Pendleton Elementary.

In happier times she enjoyed riding with her father, Dr. Robert Bolt Day, to make house calls. Upon their return, she would relate—with a mixture of fright and fun—how the car slipped and slid over the country clay roads.

On other days she and her younger sister Katharine played baseball with their older brothers, Robert Eugene and Elias. Knowing they were allowed to play only because more team members were needed never dampened their spirits.

But now, as Robert Eugene—who was five years older—sat beside Nancy Jane holding a schoolbook, it was not in fun. He was intent on helping his sister keep up with her class while she was out with measles.

Nancy Jane's father and her mother, Kate Eskew Day, emphasized books, always including them in the celebrations of birthdays and Christmases. Thus, the children loved to read. Dr. Day also pulled his children into discussions of world affairs during mealtime.

Nancy Jane and Elias claimed, as children will, that the two of them, as middle children, were not family favorites like Robert, the oldest and the apple of his mother's eye, or Katharine, the baby. Still, they had to admit that with a set of grandparents close by they all were spoiled.

In spite of the family's close relationship, the children received no sympathy—especially from their parents—the *one* day they played hooky from school.

With school, paper dolls, ball games and books, Nancy Jane found time passing quickly in her small hometown of Pendleton. Only the death of her father when she was sixteen marred an otherwise happy youth.

Her father's death, too, caused her to choose a college closer to her home—Greenville Woman's College. Upon graduation, she took a teaching position in Winston-Salem, North Carolina. From being a middle-school teacher, she moved into library service.

After a time of librarianship at her alma mater and Greenville Public Library, Nancy Jane received and accepted an offer in the library at Florida State College for Women.

In 1939 Nancy Jane again returned to South Carolina to instruct students at Winthrop in library science.

To earn a master's degree in library science, she attended the University of Michigan, where she graduated in 1943. She then served as an assistant professor at Emory University in Atlanta for the next three years.

For a long time librarians over South Carolina had been stressing the need for a supervisor of library services in the public schools. In 1946 the state Department of Education received a grant to fill this need. Thus, Nancy Jane Day became South Carolina's first State Librarian over black and white schools.

Miss Day had always felt fortunate to work under and with excellent librarians during her career thus far, and she found the state position surrounded by well wishers and educators deeply committed to the development of libraries. All gave their best in service and in upgrading library education.

Family Photo

Nancy Jane smiles to remember that when she made odd requests of her coworkers, they were never critical of her. Instead, one might say, "Now why do you suppose the state department wants us to do that?"

In 1953 when Nancy Jane had the honor of going to the University of Chulalongkorn in Thailand as a Fulbright Lecturer, York High School Librarian Nancy Burge filled in for her in the state Department of Education.

During Nancy Jane's twenty-four years as supervisor of library services for the Department of Education, she made outstanding accomplishments. A major achievement came with the establishment of elementary school libraries in the state. She also worked closely with colleges for library education and instigated a study to show the need for a school of graduate study in library science at the University of South Carolina. Observing that many classroom teachers went into library science, she pointed out that these teachers needed graduate courses in making this transition. She served on a committee to work toward this goal. All members found great satisfaction when their dream was realized.

Miss Day served on many professional boards and held offices, including presidencies, in numerous associations. Among them were the Council of the American Library Association, Board of Education for Librarianship, American Association of School Librarians, the Southeastern Library Association, the South Carolina Library Association, the American Association of University Women, the Association of Supervisors and Curriculum Development, the Delta Kappa Gamma Society, the American Association of University Women, and the South Carolina Council for Common Good.

Miss Day was also on the Executive Committee Tennessee Valley Library Council for Southeastern States Cooperative Survey. She holds a life membership in the National Education Association and has contributed articles to professional journals.

Miss Day was active in civic affairs such as the League of Women Voters. She is listed in *Who's Who in America, Who's Who in Library Service,* and *Who's Who in the South and Southeast.*

Furman University honored her with the Mary Sullivan Award in 1963. The Association of School Librarians established a scholarship in her name.

Presently Miss Day and her sister Katharine make their home in Laurens.

Elizabeth Boatwright Coker

AUTHOR
1909–1993

Teen-age Elizabeth glanced out of the classroom window. She ached with boredom. The study of Latin with its dull repetition was just too much.

"All right, Elizabeth," her teacher called to her, "translate the next part."

Not even looking at the right page, Elizabeth naturally recited something totally incorrect. Her punishment was to stay after school and write a poem.

For the imaginative mind of Elizabeth, this was no punishment. The poem she wrote was "Noches," Spanish for *night*. It was about two horsemen who were returning from a rodeo. Her principal was so impressed with her creativity she entered the poem in a national poetry contest for high school students. It won first place and hooked Elizabeth on writing.

Born April 21, 1909, in Darlington, to Purves Jenkins and Bessie Heard Boatwright, Elizabeth was always a child with a poetic, mystical nature. She loved making up rhymes and putting her imaginative touches on everything around her. She even named her pony Bo-nail because he stepped on her toenail.

In spite of the typical teasing of two older brothers, her childhood was a happy one with lots of friends. She loved animals, birds, the theater, and dancing. In fact, at one time she aspired to be a dancer, even winning a statewide contest at Myrtle Beach by doing the Charleston. But it was another ambition that she explored more thoroughly—that of being a poet. During her high school years she won several scholastic awards, national as well as regional.

Converse College

Elizabeth Boatwright Coker in 1989

When Elizabeth was fifteen, she underwent a difficult time in her life. A car wreck crushed the right side of her face, knocking out teeth and breaking her jawbone. For a time she suffered great despair. She refused to go out of their home because of her swollen, disfigured face.

It was her father's wisdom that finally helped her to cope. One afternoon he insisted she ride with him in their open touring car. When they neared the main street, Elizabeth got in the foot of the car to avoid being seen.

"You *will* get up," her father said, and she had no choice but to obey. But to Elizabeth's amazement, familiar faces called out friendly greetings to her. Friends loved her for herself, not her looks.

It is still a medical miracle that Elizabeth healed so beautifully. In fact, at the end of World War II, Edward R. Murrow invited her to be a guest on his radio show. He used the interview to encourage young men returning from war with facial injuries.

At Converse College Elizabeth continued her interest in poetry. She was editor of *The Concept,* the school's literary magazine, and won numerous honors for her poetry, including the Skylark Prize, awarded by the Poetry Society of South Carolina. She also published in national magazines such as *Harper's* and *Saturday Evening Post.*

After college Elizabeth went to New York with aspirations to work on the *New York Times.* Instead, she ended up modeling hats and shoes. Later, however, she worked for Dell Publications.

Perhaps the most significant event of her New York period was meeting James Lide Coker, III, a recent graduate of Harvard Business School and her future husband. To her surprise, he was also from South Carolina—from a place only fifteen miles from her hometown.

The two married in 1930 and lived in Hartsville, where her husband was a business executive. It was here her husband's grandfather had established Coker College.

For a time Elizabeth's writing was superseded by other interests. She did graduate study at Middleburg College in Vermont and brought up their children, James Lide Coker, IV, and Penelope. She often referred to this period as a "time to live and grow up."

When Elizabeth did return to her writing—for she always knew she would—it was to prose rather than the poetry of her earlier years. *Daughter of Strangers,* a novel of historical fiction, was published in 1950. In this work she focused on events and people in the days leading to the Civil War. The book showed her keen knowledge of Southern plantation life—the cotton-field songs, horse breeding, slave dialect, and other aspects of South Carolina life during the pre–Civil War. The book stayed on the *New York Times* best-seller list for six months.

Her first novel set the pace for others. Following in succession were *The Day of the Peacock, India Allan, The Big Drum, La Belle, Lady Rich, The Bees, Blood Red Roses,* and *The Grasshopper King.*

Often inspired by diaries written by her own grandmother and others, Mrs. Coker did extensive research for each novel. Research took her as far as England, Mexico, and even on a safari in Kenya, East Africa. Most often she drew on the history of South Carolina and blended those events with characters from her heart. Always evident is a sense of fair play and a genuine concern for the underdog. And, because of her love of horses, she wrote about them.

Mrs. Coker's books have been translated into several languages. In 1973 she wrote "This Is Billy Boy," her gift to the South Carolina Association for Retarded Children.

Among honors for her writing Mrs. Coker won international short story awards from PEN and Author's Guild. She participated in many literary conferences and served as a lecturer in various colleges. She was a visiting professor of English at Appalachian State University.

She was a member of the Poetry Society of South Carolina, the National Board of Woman's Medical College, International Social Service and World Adoption Fund, and the Hartsville School Board, and she served as director of United Cerebral Palsy of South Carolina. She also devoted time to hospital work.

Mrs. Coker traveled extensively—always with her husband until his death in 1963.

As romantic as her heroines, Elizabeth Boatwright Coker was a picture of femininity. Underneath her gracious dignity and charming Southern accent was one who enjoyed rainy nights, sweet-smelling flowers, walking in the woods, and good conversation. She loved ballads and folk music; a favorite was "Black Is the Color of My True Love's Hair."

Mrs. Coker, hailed by Jonathan Daniels as South Carolina's First Lady of Letters, died September 1, 1993. She is buried in Magnolia Cemetery in Hartsville.

Augusta Baker

STORYTELLER
1911–

"Read to me! Read to me!"

Tiny Augusta, book in hand, tagged behind her mother in their Baltimore, Maryland, home.

Her constant demand to be read to sometimes made Augusta a pest. Yet, even an occasional reprimand for her belligerent insistence did not deter her. And Augusta usually won the desire of her heart—the sharing of a story.

The story, however, must be told exactly right. Never did she allow her busy mother to substitute one word for another or to shorten a story so she could hurry back to her many tasks.

"That's not the way the story goes," she would say imperiously.

Augusta's parents could understand their only child's love for books. Both teachers, Winfort J. and Mabel Gough Braxston were a "book family."

Born on April 1, 1911, Augusta couldn't remember when her life did not center on books or the stories told by her grandmother. Hour after hour the wonderful storyteller would occupy her energetic granddaughter with imaginative tales.

As Augusta grew older, books continued to hold a major place in her life. She loved her teachers and enjoyed school. One of her fondest memories is listening to an elementary teacher reading aloud from *Beautiful Joe,* a book about a dog. Each Friday the class would hear a chapter relating the trials of the poor animal. Always the cliff-hanging end of the reading would leave Augusta with a mixture of anguish and anticipation until the next week, when the story would continue.

Family Photo

Not even her love of roller-skating kept her from her books for very long.

After graduation from high school, Augusta found that studies at the University of Pittsburgh whetted her appetite for folklore. Later at Albany State Teachers' College, now New York State University, she continued her education as Mrs. James Baker, II. There she studied under a leading New York state folklorist.

The couple continued to make their home in Albany, where James opened a branch of the Urban League. By 1934 Augusta had graduated and James, at the request of President Franklin Roosevelt, was transferred to New York to head up the Home Relief Bureau of the Urban League.

It was in New York in 1939 that Mrs. Baker began her career as a children's librarian in the New York Public Library. In short order she found that she must be able to tell stories.

"Storytelling," the other librarians told her, "is a way of bringing children and books together." After all, that *was* the purpose of a children's library.

"My career *really* began," Augusta Baker said, "the day I was sent to 135th Street Branch to work with the children of Harlem."

Improving the black image for children and ridding books of stereotypical presentations of blacks became one of her main concerns.

Intent on her goal, Mrs. Baker did research in the field of black literature for children. She founded a special collection for children housed at the Countee Cullen Branch of the New York Public Library.

In 1953 as a result of her contributions Mrs. Baker was appointed storytelling specialist for more than eighty library branches and later the Central Office coordinator of children's services.

During this time Mrs. Baker edited the books *Readings for Children, Talking Tree, Young Years, The Golden Lynx,* and *Once Upon a Time.* She also compiled a list of titles that was published by the New York Public Library as *The Black Experience in Children's Books.* The bibliography, regarded as a landmark publication in its field, has gone through several editions and revisions. It is now nationally known.

For her research Mrs. Baker received the first Dutton-Macrae Award from the American Library Association.

Because she thought the portrayal of minorities in children's books was demeaning, she began a campaign to get black writers to write for children and to look for illustrators who would draw true representations of blacks.

She inaugurated a weekly radio broadcast, "The World of Children's Literature." She also served as a consultant and bibliographer for the television program "Sesame Street."

Mrs. Baker has done workshops and taught in the schools of library services in Syracuse, Columbia, and Rutgers universities. She retired from her work with the New York Public Library in 1974, but she has continued to conduct seminars and serve as visiting lecturer at colleges and universities around the country. She also acts as a consultant in the area of children's work.

In 1977 Mrs. Baker served as co-editor with Ellin Greene for *Storytelling: Art and Technique.*

For her contribution to children and children's literature, as well as to librarianship, Mrs. Baker has received numerous awards. Among them are the Parents' Magazine Medal, the American Library Association Grolier Award, the Constance Lindsay Skinner Award, and ALA Honorary Life Membership, the Regina Award from the National Catholic Library Association, honorary doctorates from St. John's University in Jamaica, New York, and from the University of South Carolina, as well as the Nelson A. Rockefeller Award from the State University of New York in Albany.

"The best reward for it all," says Mrs. Baker, "is to have children settle in their seats, fix their eyes on the storyteller, and wait for her to say, 'Once upon a time . . .' "

Currently Mrs. Baker serves as "Storyteller-in-Residence" for the University of South Carolina's College of Library and Information Science. Her job, she says, is to train adults to tell stories.

"The impact storytellers have on children is tremendous," she says. "We never forget adults who told us stories or read to us when we were children."

Mrs. Baker sincerely believes that storytelling is filled with educational and cultural values. Not only does it expose children to quality literature and to the beauty of spoken language, but it also builds listening skills.

Each year an "A (ugusta) Baker's Dozen—A Celebration of Stories" is held in Columbia. "We are never too old to be read to," Mrs. Baker says, "for good reading aloud is storytelling." The two-day event honors this world-renowned, master storyteller.

Mrs. Baker lives in Columbia, where she enjoys a close relationship with her son's family while still pursuing her lifelong dream—*the sharing of a story.*

Juanita Redmond Hipps

ARMY NURSE
1913–1979

"Where are you hurt, soldier?" Juanita Redmond leaned close to the stretcher and strained under a night sky to see one of the many wounded men being brought in from the jungle to the makeshift hospital on Bataan.

Receiving no answer, she picked up his wrist. There was no pulse.

Juanita Redmond, a native of Swansea, South Carolina, was serving as a nurse in the Philippines during World War II. After a bombing raid, the hospital staff worked through the night giving injections to relieve pain, cutting away bloody clothing, removing shrapnel, stitching wounds, amputating, and covering the wounded they could not save.

Juanita and the other nurses took a personal interest in the wounded soldiers so far from home. They saved cardboard to cut into playing cards and jigsaw puzzles to help them while away the long hours. And whenever possible, they found humor among the tragedies. Always Juanita was touched by the soldiers' appreciation. Even the prisoners of war appeared grateful for their decent treatment.

As a young nursing graduate of the State Hospital School of Nursing in Columbia, South Carolina, Juanita entered the Army Nurse Corp in 1936. When the Japanese bombed Pearl Harbor on December 7, 1941, she was stationed at Sternberg General Hospital in Manila. With most of the American aircraft destroyed on the ground, Japanese troops poured into the Philippine Islands. Without air cover, the American and Filipino soldiers were pushed back. Soon the Japanese captured all of Luzon, the main island, except for the Bataan Peninsula. It was there and to the island of Corregidor that Juanita and other Americans retreated just before Christmas. The troops held out for many months until they were finally hemmed in and cut off from supplies. In spite of the huge red crosses painted on sheets and rooftops, bombs fell constantly. Food was nearly gone, and the number of casualties grew bigger daily.

Since white nurses' uniforms could be spotted by the enemy—even in the moonlight—nurses wore khaki shirts and trousers, helmets, and GI shoes.

When "Red," as she was sometimes called, was not working among the soldiers or in the operating room, she was in charge of the kitchen. The first thing wounded soldiers asked for on being brought in was food. In spite of dwindling supplies, Juanita would always manage to find something for them.

Lt. Juanita Redmond stands next to Mrs. Franklin Roosevelt at a ceremony honoring Army nurses of Bataan.

As bombs and shrapnel fell, off-duty nurses dived into foxholes; those on duty stretched out on the floor between their patients' cots until the bombing was over and they could get back to work.

On Easter morning Juanita was working on the wards when a shout, "Planes overhead!" rang out. A bomb fell close, knocking her down. She managed to pull herself up and help cut patients' traction ropes so they could roll onto the floor. Another bomb whined, and she was knocked to the floor again. From the ward a voice called, "Where's Miss Redmond? Is Miss Redmond all right?" Juanita recognized the voice. It belonged to a soldier who had lost both legs.

General Jonathan Wainwright, having received the command of Bataan from General Douglas MacArthur, ordered Juanita and other nurses to the island of Corregidor. It was with much sorrow that Juanita left behind the men she had come to love.

In their flight to Corregidor, they frequently had to take refuge in ditches alongside the road. When this happened, weariness would overcome them immediately, and they would fall asleep. Finally they reached their destination.

The hospital in Corregidor was housed in the Malinta Tunnel, made in the heart of a great rock, yet the personnel continued to face attacks by the Japanese. The bombings became more frequent, and the plight of homeless refugees wrenched the hearts of those trying to help.

When it was clear that the Japanese would soon invade the island, Juanita and the other nurses were again ordered to leave their posts—this time for Melbourne, Australia. It was like leaving Bataan all over again. She knew what the end for those left behind would be like. She had no choice but to follow orders, yet she felt like a deserter. Even though the odds were against their ever reaching Australia, the evacuation was successful.

From there the nurses were taken to San Francisco, where their first assignment was to talk to the families of men who were stationed on the doomed islands. "In a way," Juanita said, "telling parents and wives about their boys was harder than anything on Bataan or Corregidor." There, at least she had been able to sleep from exhaustion rather than lie awake remembering the tragedies. Some family members brought photographs, hoping to hear that the loved ones were still alive; others sought comfort. Sometimes the nurses could only say "He died like a good soldier."

Along with the other nurses who escaped, Juanita received the Purple Heart "for conspicuous bravery under fire." She also received the National Defense and the Pacific and Asiactic Theatre ribbons set with combat stars, the Presidential Unit Citation ribbon with stars for Bataan and Corregidor, the Philippine Defense ribbon, and the Bronze Star. Juanita was one of the first nurses to earn her golden flight wings.

Upon her return to the states, she was featured on the Ed Sullivan Show. On July 13, 1942, she was given a hero's welcome with a parade in Columbia.

Juanita Redmond is the author of *I Served on Bataan*. The book was used as the background for the World War II movie "So Proudly We Hail." She helped establish the flight nurse program for the United States Air Corps.

At the time of her retirement in 1946 she was acting chief of the Air Force Nurse Corps and a lieutenant colonel.

Juanita was married to Brigadier General William G. Hipps. The couple had a son, William G. Hipps, Jr.

Lieutenant Colonel Juanita Redmond Hipps died in Saint Petersburg, Florida. She was sixty-six. Burial took place in Arlington National Cemetery with full military honors.

Althea Gibson

TENNIS CHAMPION
1927–

"Put up your dukes!"

Thirteen-year-old Althea knew she had better get ready to defend herself against her daddy's punches and jabs, or she would get a beating.

For a long time Althea had been convinced that her daddy wanted a boy for his first child. "You're big and strong, Althea," he would say. "There's no reason why you can't be a woman boxer. Haven't I taught you the footwork and how to block punches?"

Daniel Gibson just couldn't seem to get it through his head that Althea didn't want to be a prizefighter. Oh, he had taught her to defend herself all right, and Althea needed that to grow up in a place like Harlem.

Tall, muscular Althea didn't have any trouble establishing a reputation for being able to defend herself. In fact, she normally managed to get in the first punch. She didn't fight just girls who picked on her, but boys too. And they fought back with fists, elbows, knees, and sometimes teeth.

Even though Althea was a fighter, she never got into any real trouble. She was bad, though, about playing hooky from school. The only thing Althea wanted to do was play ball. She felt she was wasting time in the classroom when she could be shooting baskets at the playground.

Althea's daddy whipped her hard about staying out of school, but he never could make her go regularly and behave the way her younger brother and three sisters did.

Sometimes when Althea's mother would send her on an errand to the store, she would start playing stickball with the boys in the street and forget all about the loaf of bread or the quart of milk. At dark she knew she didn't dare go home, where she would get a good beating, so she would spend the money on something else and take off for a couple of days on one of her hooky sprees.

One time when she had stayed out late, she went to a place on Fifth Avenue called the Society for the Prevention of Cruelty to Children.

"I'm scared to go home," she told the lady. "My father will whip me something awful."

Bing Studio, Harper & Row

Althea stayed there for a while, but her fighting got her into solitary confinement. When she returned home, it was with the warning that if she got into any more trouble, she would be sent to a girls' correctional school.

In spite of all the beatings her father gave her, Althea knew he loved her and was trying his best to bring her up right.

Although Althea couldn't remember Silver, the small town in South Carolina where she was born on August 25, 1927, her father used to tell her about the times there when she was a little tot. They shot "marbles" in the dirt road, he said, using acorns for marbles. He told her, too, that he would like nothing better than to go back to Silver and raise chickens on the old farm place he used to sharecrop.

But Althea didn't feel the way her daddy did about South Carolina. As far as she was concerned, the South was a place where they forced blacks to sit in the rear of the bus and made them feel ashamed about not being allowed to eat at lunch counters.

I won't ever go back to the South to live," Althea would say, "until things change."

Her daddy, now a handyman in a garage, would point to the slum tenements with the plaster falling down and the plumbing stopped up and to the kids getting killed in the streets. "Is this better?" he would ask.

Living on Manhattan's swarming 143rd Street and being poor didn't bother Althea all that much. She could always scrounge around for empty bottles to trade in for a bottle of soda. Besides, the thing she liked most about their neighborhood was the Police Athletic League Play Street. The police would put up wooden barricades to close off streets to traffic so the kids could play paddle tennis and shuffleboard.

Althea, with her long arms and giant stride, was the champion of the block. With the wooden rackets they used, she could really swat the sponge rubber or tennis balls.

A musician, Buddy Walker, who worked for the city as a play leader, recognized Althea's talent and bought her a second-hand tennis racket. Later he took her to tennis courts in Harlem to play with his friends. He also arranged for Althea to play at the Cosmopolitan Club, where she had the club's one-armed professional, Fred Johnson, as an instructor.

At first the polite manners of tennis seemed silly to Althea. All she wanted to do was play the game, not study how to be a fine lady.

She had trouble, too, as a competitor because she wanted to fight the player who was beating her in a match. She once started to the stands to beat up a spectator who made remarks about her.

After a while, though, she began to understand that a person could walk out on the court like a lady all dressed in white, be polite, and still beat the "liver and lights out of a ball."

Althea's real break came in 1946 when two Southern doctors saw her play tennis in a tournament sponsored by the American Tennis Association. It was their idea that she would go to college and play tennis.

When they told Althea their plans, she replied, "That would be great if I'd ever been to high school."

Nevertheless, Dr. Robert W. Johnson of Lynchburg, Virginia, and Dr. Hubert A. Eaton of Wilmington, North Carolina, agreed to take Althea home with them, letting her live with each family part of the year.

Returning to the South was not an easy decision for Althea. She had heard stories about the treatment of blacks there. What would it be like living in a small town? Harlem wasn't any heaven, but at least she knew how to get along in the city.

Encouraged to go by her idol, Sugar Ray Robinson, Althea packed her few belongings and her saxaphone, given to her by Sugar Ray, and set out. The

Eatons and the Johnsons lived up to all they had promised and more. They couldn't have treated Althea more like one of their own. They enrolled her in Williston Industrial High School in Wilmington, where she joined the band and became a member of a little jazz combo. She also became captain of the basketball team.

Even all that and the tennis practices with the doctors was not enough, however, to keep Althea occupied. Much to the dismay of the other girls, she would go out to the field and play baseball and football with the boys.

With the doctors looking out for her, Althea played in tournaments. Sometimes she was the only black.

When Althea graduated from high school in 1949, she received a scholarship to Florida Agricultural and Mechanical University in Tallahassee. There she played on the basketball and tennis teams.

During this time Althea traveled to some American Tennis Association tournaments. She won the women's singles three years in a row. She was also the first black to compete in the singles championship at Forest Hills, Long Island.

In 1951 Althea was one of four American tennis players to be sent on a good-will tour of Asia.

In July of 1957, Althea scored her first major United States tennis victory by defeating Darlene Hard in the National Clay Court Championships. In September she won the United States National Women's grass court title at Forest Hills. She was also selected to represent the United States in Women's Wightman Cup Tennis Matches in Sewickley, Pennsylvania.

The Associated Press poll voted Althea Gibson Outstanding Woman Athlete of that year. Other highlights included meeting Queen Elizabeth, being greeted with a ticker-tape parade in New York, and being asked to sing on television's *Ed Sullivan Show.*

In Althea's Wimbledon speech she gave credit to all the people who had helped her become the champion women's tennis player of the world. Among those cited was her coach, Sydney Llewellyn.

Althea has said of herself, "Some people think I am a cold person underneath, but I'm not. Perhaps I act that way sometimes because I grew up a suspicious loner. I was withdrawn and slow to trust any part of myself to other people."

There is no feeling of exclusion any more for Althea Gibson. Instead, there has been much good will.

Even though Althea was often bitterly disappointed in defeat, she never gave up to the point that she wanted to hang up her racket. This Harlem Street paddle tennis champion went all the way to the top in tennis, a sport that is traditionally dominated by players from the more affluent private clubs.

South Carolina is proud to claim Althea Gibson. In 1983 she was inducted into the South Carolina Athletic Hall of Fame.

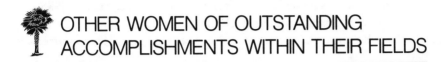

OTHER WOMEN OF OUTSTANDING ACCOMPLISHMENTS WITHIN THEIR FIELDS

Actresses

Ada, Clare. b. Charleston, 1836. Actress, author.

Jaffe, Bettye Ackerman. b. Williston, 1924. Theater, movies, television.

Kitt, Eartha. b. North, 1928. Entertainer, singer.

Kramer, Mary Lou. b. Millen, Ga., 1907. Teacher, director Children's Theater. d. 1988.

McClendon, Rose. b. Greenville, 1884. Actress. d. 1936.

McKiney, Nina Mae. b. Lancaster, 1912. Actress, singer, bandleader. d. 1967.

Woodward, Joanne. b. Thomasville, Ga., 1930. Movies, television.

Artists

Dupré, Grace Annette. b. Spartanburg, 1894. Portraitist, musician. d. 1984.

Legare, Mary Swinton. b. Charleston, 1792. Landscape painter. d. c. 1843.

Richardson, Anne Worsham. b. Turbeville, 1922. Artist-naturalist.

Taylor, Anna Heyward. b. Columbia, 1879. Artist. d. 1956.

Waring, Leila. b. Charleston., 1876. Miniature painter. d. 1964.

Wells, Sabina Elliott. b. Charleston, 1876. Painter. d. 1943.

Authors

Blackwell, Harriet Gray. b. Laurens, 1898. Poet, musician.

Ballard, Mignon Franklin. b. Calhoun, Ga., 1934. Editor, author of juveniles, mysteries.

Boling, Katharine Singleton. b. Florence, 1933. Writer, educator.

Byars, Betsy. b. Charlotte, N.C., 1928. Juvenile books.

Causey, Elizabeth (Beth) Green. b. West Point, Miss., 1924. Editor, publisher, historian, author of Carolina material for elementary schools.

Childress, Alice. b. Charleston, 1920. Poet, novelist, playwright, actress, editor.

Dowling, Edith Bannister. b. Liverpool, England, 1915. Poet, educator.

Dubose, Louise Jones. b. Columbus, Ga., 1901. Author, editor, teacher, d. 1985.

Few, Mary Dodgen. b. Spartanburg, 1912. Historical novels.

Freeman, Grace Beacham. b. Spartanburg, 1916. Poet Laureate of South Carolina for 1985.

Gilman, Caroline Howard. b. Boston, Mass., 1794. Editor, writer. d. 1888.

Grosvenor, Verta Mae. b. Fairfax, 1938. Writer.

Halford, Celia Childress. b. Columbia, 1942. Educator, artist, author of juveniles and fiction.

Henning, Helen Kohn. b. North Carolina. Author, historian. d. 1961.

Head, Ann (Anne Christensen Morse). b. Beaufort, 1915. Fiction. d. 1968.

Humphries, Josephine. b. Charleston, 1945. Novelist, educator.

Hyer, Helen von Kolnitz. b. Charleston, 1892. Poet Laureate of South Carolina for 1974–83. d. 1983.

Johnson, Barbara Ferry. b. Grosse Pointe, Mich., 1923. Novelist, educator. d. 1989.

Jones, Katharine Macbeth. b. Greenville, 1899. Author, historian, librarian. d. 1977.

King, Helen. b. Newberry County, 1916. Poetry, nonfiction, fiction.

Klosky, Beth Ann. b. Anderson, 1912. Journalist, editor, historian, biographer, lecturer.

Ludvigson, Susan. b. Rice Lake, Wis., 1942. Poet, educator.

Lumpkin, Grace. b. Milledgeville, Ga., 1901. Novelist. d. 1980.

Massey, Mary Elizabeth D. b. Morrilton, Ark., 1915. Historical writings.

McKinney, Jean Bradham. b. Batesburg, 1914. Poetry, prose, plays.

Mims, Frances. b. Union, 1921. Author, educator.

Moise, Penina. b. Charleston, 1797. Jewish hymns. d. 1880.

Nealy, Bertha West. b. Pageland, 1893. Poet. d. 1987.

Neuffer, Irene. b. Columbia, 1919. Journalist, author.

Osborne, Anne Riggs. b. Washington, D.C., 1922. Novelist, historian.

Parish, Peggy, b. Manning, 1927. Juvenile author. d. 1988.

Ravenel, Beatrice Witte. b. Charleston, 1870. Author, poet. d. 1956.

Rhyne, Nancy. b. Mt. Holly, N.C., 1926. Ghost stories, plantation tales, murder mysteries, juvenile books.

Ripley, Katharine Ball. b. Charleston, 1899. Author.

Roberts, Nancy Correll. b. South Milwaukee, Wis., 1924. Author, editor, publisher.

Sinclair, Bennie Lee. b. Greenville, 1939. Fiction, Poet Laureate of South Carolina 1987–.

Simons, Katharine D. Mayrant. b. Charleston, 1890. Historical novelist.

Sloan, Kathleen Lewis. b. Winnsboro. Author, director of USC Press.

Steedman, Marguerite Couturier. b. Atlanta, Ga., 1908. Author, journalist.

Tate, Eleanora. b. Canton, Mo., 1948. Journalist, editor, juvenile author.

Wells, Helena. b. Charleston, 1757. Fiction, nonfiction. First South Carolina novelist. d. 1824.

Educators

Anderson, Mary Augusta Crow. b. Sumter, 1922. Educator, author.

Bonham, Annie E. b. Edgefield County, 1856. Educator. d. 1921.

Bostick, Lucy Hampton. b. Columbia, 1898. Librarian, publisher. d. 1969.

Boyd, Rosamonde Ramsey. b. Durham, N.C., 1900. Educator, author.

Burge, Nancy. b. York, 1910. Educator, librarian. First teacher of library science at University of South Carolina.

Childs, Arney R. b. Asheville, N.C., 1891. Educator, civic leader. d. 1987.

Cone, Dr. Bonnie E. b. Lodge, 1907. Educator, university president. d. 1978.

Dacus, Ida Jane. b. Williamston, 1875. Librarian, Winthrop College. d. 1964.

Davis, Dr. Marianna White. b. Philadelphia, Pa., 1929. Educator, author.

Dial, Rebecca. b. Laurens County, 1894. Librarian, author.

Dillard, Irene Elliott. b. Laurens County, 1893. U.S.C's first dean of women, U.S.C's first full professorship. d. 1978.

Ebaugh, Laura Smith. b. Greenville, 1898. Educator, historian, librarian.

Faunt, Joan Reynolds. b. Columbia, 1918. Researcher, librarian. d. 1969.

Frayser, Mary Elizabeth. b. Virginia, 1875. Educator, pioneer in women's rights and social work. d. 1968.

Gee, Mary Wilson, b. Spartanburg, 1874. Dean d. 1963.

Hall, Ellen Wood. b. Pulaski, Va., 1945. President of Converse College, 1989.

Hartin, Theo. b. East Flat Rock, North Carolina, 1910. Educator, founder of kindergarten.

Hite, Mary Eva. b. Batesburg, 1888. Organizer of forerunner of PTA. d. 1977.

Jenkins, Barbara Williams. b. Union. 1934. Librarian, State College.

Judson, Mary Camille. b. Greenville, c. 1838. Pioneer in higher education. d. 1920.

Moses, Kathleen Johnson. b. Hope Mills, 1918. Librarian.

Mosimann, Madeline. b. Charleston, 1914. Librarian.

Piper, Martha Kime. b. Salem, Va., 1932. President of Winthrop College. d. 1988.

Spain, Frances Lander. b. Jacksonville, Fla., 1903. Librarian, educator.

Stackhouse, Eunice Ford. b. Blenheim, 1884. Educator, pioneer in race relations.

Tolbert, Marguerite. b. Laurens. 1893. Educator. d. 1982.

Walker, Estellene Paxton. b. Bristol, Va., 1911. Director of State Library, developed public libraries in S.C. d. 1984.

Withers, Sarah. b. Chester, 1873. Teacher, author. d. 1955.

Wright, Elizabeth Evelyn. b. Talbotton, Ga., 1872. Founder of Voorhees College, Denmark, S.C. d. 1906.

Yeargin, Mary L. b. Laurens County, 1867. Educator. d. 1893.

Government/Women's Rights

Edson, Anita Pollitzer. b. Charleston, c. 1897. Leader in women's suffrage, artist. d. 1981.

Perry, "Jim" Margrave. b. Greenville, c. 1886. First woman admitted to legal practice in South Carolina. d. 1963.

Salley, Eulalee Chafee, b. Augusta, Ga., 1883. Leader in women's suffrage. d. 1975.

Smith, Francis Harrison, b. Columbia, 1919. Clerk of S.C. Supreme Court.

Tucker, Cornelia Dabney. b. Asheville, N.C., 1881. Pioneer in women's rights, instrumental in obtaining secret ballot for South Carolina.

Van Exem, Elizabeth Gasque. b. 1886. South Carolina's first U.S. Congresswoman. Elected in 1938 to complete husband's term. d. 1989.

Watson, Inez. b. Anderson County, 1907. First female clerk of South Carolina House of Representatives, editor of South Carolina Legislative Manual d. 1989.

Young, Virginia Durant. b. Marion County, 1842. Pioneer for women's rights, journalist, speaker, novelist. d.1906.

Women Who Served in the General Assembly

Senate - Mary G. Ellis. (D) Jasper County. 1929–32. First woman to be elected to the Senate in regular general election and to serve full term.

House - Harriet Frazier Johnson. (D) York County. 1945–46.

House - Emma Jane McDermott. (D) York County. 1953–54.

House - Martha T. Fitzgerald. (D) Richland County. 1951–62. First woman to be elected to the House in regular election and to serve full term.

House - Ruby G. Wesson. (D) Spartanburg County. 1959–60.

House - Virginia Gourdin. (D) Charleston County. 1959–62.

House - Ruth Williams. (D) Charleston County. 1963–64.

House - Carolyn E. Frederick. (R) Greenville County. 1967–76.

Senate - Thomasine Grayson Mason. (D) Dist. 20 Clarendon and Sumter counties. 1967–68.

House - Sherry Shealy. (R) Lexington County. 1971–74.

Senate - Sherry Shealy Martschink. (R) Elected Apr. 21, 1987.

House - Irene K. Rudnick. (D) Aiken County. 1973–78; 1981–84; 1987–88.

House - Norma C. Russell. (R) Lexington County. 1973–80.

Senate - Norma C. Russell. (R) Lexington County. 1981–84.

House - Jewel S. Baskin. (R) Richland County. 1973–74.

House - Juanita W. Goggins. (D) York County. 1975–80.

House - Jean H. Toal. (D) Richland County. 1975–86; 1987–Feb. 10, 1988 (Resigned upon election to Supreme Court).

House - Joyce C. Hearn. (R) Richland County. 1975–82; 1983–84; 1985–86; 1987–88.

House - Ferdinan B. (Nancy) Stevenson. (D) Charleston County. 1974–78. Elected Lt. Gov. in general election, 1978.

House - Sylvia K. Dreyfus. (D) Greenville County. 1977–78.

House- Jean B. Meyers. (D) Horry County. 1977–82.

House - M. Lois Eargle. (D) Horry County. 1977–82; 1983–84. (R) 1984.

House - Virginia L. Crocker. (D) Laurens County. 1979–1984.

House - Jean L. Harris (D) Chesterfield County. 1979–84; 1985–86; 1987–88.

House - Juanita M. White. (D) Jasper County. 1981–84; 1985–86; 1987–88.

Senate - Elizabeth J. Patterson. (D) Spartanburg County. 1981–84; 1985–Nov. 4, 1986, elected to U.S. Congress.

Senate - Nell W. Smith. (D) Pickens County. Elected Nov. 1981 to fill unexpired term of Harris P. Smith. Served through 1988.

House - Mary P. Miles. (D) Calhoun-Orangeburg-Lexington counties. 1983–84.

House - Harriet H. Keyserling. (D) Beaufort County. 1977–84; 1985-86; 1987–88.

House - Donna A. Moss. (D) Cherokee County. 1985–86; 1987–88.

House - Mrs. Denny Woodall Neilson. (D) Darlington County. 1984. Elected to fill unexpired term of John P. Gardner, Jr. 1985–86; 1987–88.

House - Sara V. Shelton. (D) Greenville County. 1985–86; 1987–88.

House - Lucille S. Whipper. (D) Charleston County. 1986–88.

House - Carole C. Wells. (R) Spartanburg County. 1987–88.

House - Candy Y. Waites. (D) Richland County. Elected 1988 to fill unexpired term of Jean H. Toal.

Health

Brown, Dr. Lucy Hughes, b. North Carolina, 1863. First black doctor to practice medicine in South Carolina. d. 1911.

Callan, Maude. b. Quincy, Fla., 1900. First black nurse midwife. d. 1941.

Gantt, Dr. Rosa Hirschmann. b. Camden, 1875. One of South Carolina's first women doctors and Medical Association members. d. 1935.

Gee, Christine South. b. Laurens, 1884. Pioneer in nutrition.

Guignard, Dr. Jane Bruce. b. Aiken County, 1876. One of South Carolina's first women doctors. d. 1963.

Littlejohn, Nina. b. 1879. Hospital administrator. d. 1963.

Mann, Celia. b. Charleston, slave, 1799. Midwife. d. 1867.

Pember, Phoebe Yates. b. Charleston, 1823. Civil War nurse, diarist. d. 1913.

Others

Ayers, Sarah. b. Rock Hill, 1919. Catawba Indian potter.

Barry, Margaret C. "Kate" Moore. b. 1752. Revolutionary War heroine. d. 1823.

Cannon, Harriet Starr. b. Charleston, 1823. Mother Superior of Community of St. Mary. d. 1896.

Chapin, Sally Flournoy. b. Charleston, 1830. Temperance reformer.

Conway, Marian Ann McKnight. b. Manning, 1937. Miss America, 1957.

Dreher, Jennie Taber Clarkson. b. Columbia, 1916. Patron of the arts, historic preservationist.

Edmunds, Frances Ravenel. b. Charleston, 1916. Historic preservationist.

Gramling, Betty Lane Cherry. b. Orangeburg, 1936. Miss USA, 1956.

Gridley, Mary Putnam. First female mill president in South Carolina in 1890.

Jennings, Maria Croft. b. Marion, 1886. Banking. d. 1965.

Kellogg, Clara Louise. b. Sumter, 1842. Soprano. d. 1916.

Musgrove, Mary. b. Laurens County, 1757. Patriot. d. 1780.

New River, Sally. b. near Horseshoe Bend of Sugar Creek, c. 1745. Catawba Indian queen. d. 1818.

Ramsey, Martha Laurens. b. 1759. Exemplar of colonial womanhood. d. 1811.

Rountree, Martha. b. Gainsville, Fla., 1916. Pioneer in broadcast journalism.

Townsend, Hephzibah Jenkins. b. 1780. Pioneer in religious mission in South. d. 1847.

Upton, Miriam Stevenson. b. Winnsboro, 1933. Miss Universe, 1954.

Walker, Dora Dee (Mother Walker). b. Buena Vista, Ga., 1859. First Home Demonstration agent in world. d. 1952.

Wilkinson, Marian Birnie. b. Charleston, 1870. Social Worker, founder of Wilkinson Orphanage, Cayce. d. 1956.

WOMEN RECEIVING SPECIAL RECOGNITION

S.C. Hall of Fame

1974 Dr. Wil Lou Gray
1981 Dr. Anne Austin Young
1983 Mary C. Simms Oliphant
      Mary McLeod Bethune
1985 Ann Pamela Cunningham
1986 Anna Hyatt Huntington
1992 Elizabeth Boatwright Coker

S.C. Academy of Authors

1986 Julia Peterkin
1987 Mary Boykin Chesnut
1988 Josephine Pinckney
1990 Elizabeth Boatwright Coker

S.C. Poet Laureates

1974–83 Helen von Kolnitz Hyer
1985–86 Grace Beacham Freeman
1987–   Bennie Lee Sinclair

S.C. Sports Hall of Fame

1961 Lucile Godbold
1973 Jane Crum Covington
1974 Kathryn Hemphill
1975 Carolyn Cudone
1977 Mary Shannon Wilkerson
1978 Beth Daniel
1979 Lillian Paille Seabrook
1982 Betsy Rawls
1983 Althea Gibson
1987 Jaynie Hentz

Glossary

abolish — to do away with

abolitionist — a person who wants to put an end to a law or custom

ante-bellum — before the war; specifically, the American Civil War

belles and beaux — attractive young women and men

botanist — one who studies plant life

catkin — a drooping flower that resembles a cat's tail

caul — a membrane covering the head at birth; believed by the superstitious to bring good luck

Confederate — Southern supporter of secession in the Civil War

cupola — a domelike structure

emancipation — act of setting free

floret — a small flower

"free issue" — not born into slavery

Friends — a Christian religious sect; Quakers

hod-carrier — worker who assists the bricklayer by carrying the brick and mortar in a wooden trough

horticulturist — one skilled in gardening

indigo — a blue dye obtained from plants

Ku Klux Klan — a secret society of white men who used terrorists' methods against other ethnic groups

Loyalist — a colonist who supported the British in the American Revolution

lutestring — a glossy silk cloth

marauder — one who raids and plunders

militia — any military force

mob-cap — a woman's cap, for indoor wear, with a high puffy crown

naturalist — one who studies nature by observation

pastelist — one who draws with crayons made from a paste of ground colors

patois — uncultivated speech or local dialect

Patriot — a colonist who opposed the British in the American Revolution

province — an outside territory ruled by another country

Quaker — a religious sect; Friends

Rebel — one who resists established government, such as a Confederate in the Civil War

Redcoat — name given to British soldiers during the American Revolution

Royalist — a supporter of the British during the Revolution

secession — withdrawal of southern states from the Federal Union at the start of the Civil War

tariff — taxes placed by the government

ticking — heavy cloth used for mattress and pillow covers

Tory — one who gave allegiance to Great Britain in the Revolution

tow — coarse fibers of hemp before spinning

Underground Railroad — a system set up to help slaves escape to free states and Canada

Unionist — one who supported the Federal Union of the United States during the Civil War

Yankee — a Union soldier in the Civil War

yellow jessamine — vine with funnel shaped, yellow flowers; the South Carolina state flower

zoologist — one who studies animal life

Bibliography

General References

Ellet, Elizabeth F. *Women of the American Revolution.* 3 vols. New York: Haskell House Publishers, 1969.

Guess, William Francis. *South Carolina Annals of Pride and Protest.* New York, Harper Brothers. 1960.

James, Edward T., ed. *Notable American Women, 1607–1950.* Cambridge, Mass.: Belknap Press of Harvard University, 1971.

Jones, Katharine Macbeth. *Heroines of Dixie.* New York: Bobbs-Merrill, 1955.

Leonard, Dunder, Holder, editors. *The American Woman in Colonial and Revolutionary Times, 1565–1800.* Philadelphia: University of Pennsylvania Press.

Means, Celina E. *Palmetto Stories.* New York: Macmillan, 1903.

Meriwether, James, ed. *South Carolina Women Writers.* Spartanburg, S.C.: Reprint Company, 1979.

Ramsay, David. *History of South Carolina.* 2 vols. Charleston: Longworth Company, 1809.

Ravenel, Harriot H. *Charleston, the Place and the People.* New York: Macmillan, 1906.

Spruill, Julia Cherry. *Women's Life and Work in the Southern Colonies.* Chapel Hill, N.C.: University of North Carolina Press, 1938.

Tinling, Marion. *Women Remembered: A Guide to Landmarks of Women's History in the United States.* New York: Greenwood Press, 1986.

Wallace, David D. *History of South Carolina.* 4 vols. New York: American History Society, 1934.

Wauchope, George Armstrong. *The Writers of South Carolina.* Columbia, S.C.: State Company Publishers, 1910.

Affra Harleston Coming

Jervey, T. T. "The Harlestons." *Historical Magazine,* vol. 3 (1902), p. 154.

Middleton, Margaret Simons. *Affra Harleston and Old Charles-Towne.* Columbia, S.C.: R. L. Bryan, 1971.

Henrietta Deering Johnston

Johnson, Allen, and Dumas Malone, eds. *Dictionary of American Biography.* vol. v, p. 141. New York: Charles Scribner, 1936.

Rutledge, Anna Wells. "Who Was Henrietta Johnston?" *Antiques,* March 1947, pp. 183–85.

Elizabeth Ann Timothy

Hirsch, A. H. *The Huguenots of Colonial South Carolina.* Durham, N.C.: Duke University Press, 1928.

Johnson, Allen, and Dumas Malone, eds. *Dictionary of American Biography.* vol. 9, p. 557. New York: Charles Scribner, 1936.

Witkoski, Michael. "Poor Afflicted Widow." *The State Magazine,* Feb. 9, 1986.

Hannah English Williams

"Early Letters from South Carolina upon Natural History." *Historical Magazine,* vol. 21, pp. 3–9.

Martha Daniel Logan

Hollingsworth, Buckner. *Her Garden Was Her Delight.* New York: Macmillan, 1962.

Prior, Mary B. "Letters of Martha Logan, 1760–1763." *Historical Magazine,* vol. 59 (1958), pp. 38–46.

Sophia Wigington Hume

Gummere, Amelia, ed. *The Journal and Essays of John Woolman.* New York: Macmillan, 1922.

"Mary Fisher Crosse and Sophia Hume." *Historical Magazine,* vol. 12 (1911), pp. 106–8.

Eliza Lucas Pinckney

Graydon, Nell S. *Eliza of Wappoo.* Columbia, S.C.: R. L. Bryan, 1967.

Ravenel, Harriot Horry. *Eliza Pinckney.* New York: Charles Scribner, 1896.

Williams, Frances Leigh. *Plantation Patriot.* New York: Harcourt, Brace and World, 1967.

Rebecca Brewton Motte

Harrison, Margaret Hayne. *A Charleston Album.* New Hampshire: Richard Smith Publishers, 1953.

Wister, Mrs. O. J., and Miss Agnes Irwin, eds. *Worthy Women of Our First Century.* New York: Lippincott, 1877.

Susannah Elliott

Wilson, James Grant, and John Fiske, eds. *Appleton's Cyclopedia of American Biography.* vol. 11. New York: D. Appleton and Company, 1900.

Laodicea Langston Springfield

Dubose, Louise Jones. "Three Heroines of the American Revolution." *South Carolina's Distinguished Women of Laurens County.* Columbia, S.C.: R. L. Bryan, 1972.

Green, Harry C., and Mary W. Green. *Pioneer Mothers in America.* 3 vols. New York: Putnam, 1912.

Sickels, Eleanor. *In Calico and Crinoline.* New York: Viking, 1935.

Emily Geiger

"Hilborn, Nat, and Sam Hilborn. *Battleground of Freedom.* Columbia, S.C.: Sandlapper Press, 1970.

Shealy, W. A. "Emily Geiger, a True Story of the Revolution." *The Illustrator* (Atlanta), September, 1896.

"Emily Geiger: A Heroine of the Revolution." *American Monthly Magazine,* vol. 8, March 1896.

Maria Martin

Hollingsworth, Buckner. *Her Garden Was Her Delight.* New York: Macmillan, 1962.

Williams, Margot, and Paul Elliott. "Maria Martin: The Brush Behind Audubon's Birds." *MS,* April 1977, pp. 14–18.

The Grimké Sisters

Lerner, Gerda. *The Grimké Sisters from South Carolina: Rebels Against Slavery.* Boston: Houghton Mifflin, 1967.

Willimon, William, and Patricia Willimon. *Turning the World Upside Down.* Columbia, S.C.: Sandlapper Press, 1972.

Louisa Cheves McCord

Adams, Oscar, ed. *Dictionary of American Authors.* New York: Houghton Mifflin, 1904.

Sickels, Eleanor. *In Calico and Crinoline.* New York: Viking, 1935.

Who Was Who in America: Historical Volume 1607–1896. Revised edition, p. 414. Chicago: Marquis, 1967.

Ann Pamela Cunningham

Klosky, Beth Ann. *Sandlapper Magazine,* vol. 1, August 1968, pp. 14–17ff.

Lashley, Dolores C. *Ann Pamela Cunningham: The Girl Who Saved Mount Vernon.* Columbia, S.C.: R. L. Bryan, 1982.

Lesesne, Dr. J. Mauldin. "Ann Pamela Cunningham." *Distinguished Women of Laurens County.* Columbia, S.C.: R. L. Bryan, 1972.

Lord, Clifford, ed. *Keepers of the Past.* Chapel Hill: University of North Carolina Press, 1965.

McKinney, Jean Bradham, "To Mount Vernon's Rescue." *The State Magazine,* Jan. 19, 1986.

Walworth, Ellen Hardin, ed. *American Monthly Magazine,* August 1893, pp. 201–13.

Mary Boykin Chesnut

Chesnut, Mary Boykin. *A Diary from Dixie.* Edited by Ben Ames Williams. Boston: Houghton Mifflin, 1949.

Jones, Katharine Macbeth. *Ladies of Richmond.* New York: Bobbs-Merrill, 1962.

Muhlenfeld, Elisabeth. *Mary Boykin Chesnut: A Biography.* Baton Rouge: Louisiana State University Press, 1981.

Wiley, Bell Irvin. *Confederate Women.* Westport, Conn.: Greenwood Press, 1975.

Woodward, C. Vann, ed. *Mary Chesnut's Civil War.* New Haven, Conn.: Yale University Press, 1981.

Martha Schofield

Evans, Matilda A. *Martha Schofield, Pioneer Negro Educator.* Columbia, S.C.: Dupre Printing Company, 1916.

Patterson, Mary. *Martha Schofield: Servant of the Least.* Wallingfor, Penn., 1943.

Smedley, Katherine. *Martha Schofield and the Re-education of the South, 1839–1916.* Lewiston, N.Y.: Edwin Mellen Press, 1987.

Aiken Standard & Review. March 1, 1968.

South Aiken High School Library files. Miss Lizzie Dennis, librarian.

Floride Clemson Lee

McGee, Charles M., Jr., and Ernest M. Lander, Jr., eds. *A Rebel Came Home.* Columbia, S.C.: University of South Carolina Press, 1961.

Salley, A. S., Jr. "The Calhoun Family of South Carolina." *Historical Magazine,* vol. 7 (1906), pp. 81-98, 153-169.

Elizabeth Allston Pringle

James, Edward T., ed. *Notable American Women, 1607–1950.* Cambridge, Mass.: Belknap Press of Harvard University, 1971, vol. 3, pp. 100–103.

Pennington, Patience. *A Woman Rice Planter.* New York: Macmillan, 1913.

Pringle, Elizabeth A. *Chronicles of Chicora Wood.* Boston: Christopher Publishing House, 1940.

Matilda Arabella Evans

Davis, Dr. Marianna W., Chairperson. *South Carolina's Blacks and Native Americans 1776–1976.* Columbia, S.C.: The State Human Affairs Commission, 1976.

Tindall, George Brown. *South Carolina Negroes 1877–1900.* Columbia, S.C.: University of South Carolina, 1952.

Mary McLeod Bethune

Kostman, Samuel. *Twentieth Century Women of Achievement.* New York: Richard Rosen Press, 1976.

Nathan, Dorothy. *Women of Courage.* New York: Random House 1964.

O'Shea, Margaret N. "Public Servant's Philosophy." *The State Magazine,* Oct. 7, 1979, pp. 5, 6.

Peare, Catherine Owen. *Mary McLeod Bethune.* New York: Vanguard Press, 1951.

Alice Ravenel Huger Smith

Neff, Marietta. "A Painter of the Carolina Lowlands." *The American Magazine of Art,* vol. 17, August 1926, 406-13.

Young, Gale. "Watercolorist of the Low Country." *Sandlapper Magazine,* vol. 6, pp. 32–35.

Alice Ravenel Huger Smith, A Biography. Published by her friends on her eightieth birthday. Charleston, S.C., 1956.

Anna Hyatt Huntington

A Century of American Sculpture: Treasures from Brookgreen Gardens. New York: Abbeville Press, 1988.

Brookgreen Bulletin, vol. 7, no. 3, 1983.

Brookgreen Gardens Archives.

Hornstein, Harold. "In the Heroic and Classic Mold." *Yankee,* August 1970, pp. 56–58, 104–10.

Lareau, Jane. "Beauty by the Beach." *The State Magazine,* August 24, 1986, p. 12.

Martin, Elva Cobb. "Sculpting a Garden." *The State Magazine,* May 18, 1986, pp. 4, 5.

Proske, Beatrice Gilman. *Brookgreen Garden Sculpture.* Murrells Inlet, S.C.: Brookgreen Garden Trustees, 1968, pp. 168–69.

Rogers, Winifred. "Sculptress Anna Hyatt Huntington." *Sandlapper Magazine,* May 1970, pp. 41–46.

South Caroliniana Library Collection.

Julia Mood Peterkin

Bain, Robert, Joseph M. Flora, and Louis Rubin, Jr., eds. *Southern Writers: A Biographical Dictionary.* Baton Rouge, La.: Louisiana State University Press, 1979.

Durham, Frank, ed. *Collected Short Stories of Julia Peterkin.* Columbia, S.C.: University of South Carolina Press, 1970.

Herrman, Eva. *On Parade Caricatures.* Edited by Erich Possett. New York: Coward McCann, 1929.

Landes, Thomas H. *Julia Peterkin.* Boston: Twayne Publishers, 1976.

Stackhouse Eunice Ford. "Julia Mood Peterkin." *Distinguished Women of Laurens County.* Columbia, S.C.: R. L. Bryan, 1972.

Jane Harris Hunter

Hunter, Jane. *A Nickel and a Prayer.* Cleveland, Ohio: Elli Kani Publishing, 1940.

News clippings, *Augusta Chronicle.*

Marie Cromer Seigler

Beck, Franklin. *The 4-H Story.* Ames, Iowa: The Iowa State College Press, 1951, pp. 78, 83–84.

Cooperative Extension Service, Clemson University, Clemson, S.C. Aiken files.

Griffin, Louise Huckabee. "Abbeville County Native Founder of 4-H Club Forerunner." *The Press and Banner and Abbeville Medium,* October 10, 1984.

Milner, Vivian. "Her Tomato Clubs Spread Through the Nation." *Aiken County Rambler,* Nov. 13, 1980, p. 3.

Recollections of Mrs. Helen Burckhalter, Aiken, S.C., and her friends.

South Caroliniana Library Collection.

Wessel, Thomas, and Marilyn Wessel. *4-H: An American Idea, 1900–1980.* Maryland: National 4-H Council, 1982, pp. 13–15.

Interview. Mrs. Rena Snapp, Savannah, Ga., daughter.

Elizabeth O'Neill Verner

Bussman, Marlo Pease. *Born Charlestonia.* Columbia, S.C.: State Printing Company, 1969.

Thomas, W. H. J. "Elizabeth O'Neill Verner: First Lady of Charleston." *Sandlapper Magazine,* vol. 8, December 1975, pp. 11–16.

Personal interview, June 1977.

Wil Lou Gray

Bryant, Bobby. "She Always Had a Project." *The State,* March 11, 1984.

Henderson, Ellen. "Palmetto Profiles." *Sandlapper Magazine,* May 1975.

Kohn, Erin Spence, "Dr. Wil Lou Gray." *Distinguished Women of Laurens County.* Columbia, S.C.: R. L. Bryan, 1972.

Montgomery, Mabel. *South Carolina's Wil Lou Gray.* Columbia, S.C.: Vogue Press, 1963.

"The Opportunity School Story." *The Journal* (West Columbia, 1973), p. 20.

Personal interview. June 16, 1977.

Lily Strickland

Charleston Historical Society Collection.

Howe, Anne Whitworth. *Lily Strickland: South Carolina's Gift to American Music.* Columbia, S.C.: R. L. Bryan, 1970.

Hungerpillar, J. C. *South Carolina Literature.* Columbia, S.C.: R. L. Bryan, 1931, p. 3.

Rowland, Elizabeth. "Presenting Lily Strickland." *Sandlapper Magazine,* January/February, 1975.

Slonimsky, Nicolas. *Bakers Biographical Dictionary of Musicians.* New York: Schirmer Books, 1984.

South Caroliniana Library Collection.

Walker, Cornelia G. *History of Music in South Carolina.* Columbia, S.C.: R. L. Bryan, 1958, p. 26.

Mary Gordon Ellis

Address at Meeting of Security Building and Loan Association. Columbia, S.C. March 27, 1930.

Pettus, Louise, and Ron Chepesiuk. "First Women Senator Perplexed the Men." *The Lancaster News,* March 19, 1986, p. 8–B.

Telephone interview. Mrs. Elizabeth Taylor, daughter, Greer, S.C., Feb. 20, 1989.

Mary Simms Oliphant

Hamor, Holly. "Oliphant's Books Taught South Carolina History to Generations." *Greenville Piedmont,* July 27, 1988, p. 8–A.

"Historian Joins Ranks of South Carolina Hall of Fame." *The State,* Feb. 8, 1983.

McCoin, Choice. "Personalities." *Greenville Magazine,* pp. 18–19, 60–61.

Parker, David. "Noted S. C. Historian." *The Edgefield Advertiser,* August 10, 1988, vol. 153, pp. 1, 3.

Thomas, Charles E. "South Carolina's First Lady of Letters." *Sandlapper Magazine,* January 1971, vol. 4, pp. 13–16.

Personal interview. Mrs. Alester G. Furman, III, daughter, February 1989.

Anne Austin Young

"Pioneer Woman Doctor." *Aiken Standard.* November 11, 1980, 8B.

Klosky, Beth Ann. *Daring Venture.* Columbia, S.C.: R. L. Bryan, 1978.

Klosky, Beth Ann. "Dr. Anne Austin Young." *South Carolina Distinguished Women of Laurens County.* Columbia, S.C.: R. L. Bryan, 1972.

Elizabeth White

Nicholes, Cassie. "Artist Elizabeth White." *Sandlapper Magazine.* October 1971, pp. 27-9.

Telephone interview. David Houston, S.C. Arts Commission Visual Arts Director. Feb. 27, 1989.

Twardy, Charles A. "Prolific, But Not Promoted." *The State.* December 6, 1987.

Nell Saunders Graydon

Aiken County Library Collection.

Interview. Mrs. Virginia G. Davies, daughter. Greenvood, S.C.

News clippings, *The Index-Journal.* Greenwood, S.C.

"Teller of Tall Tales," *The Columbia Record.* July 21, 1986.

Tuten, Jan. "Tales of Nell Graydon." *The State Magazine.* July 3, 1983, p. 3.

Josephine Pinckney

Charleston Historical Society Collection.

Dictionary of Literary Biography. vol. vi, 1980.

Fant, Holton J. "Charleston's Forgotten Novelist." *The State.* January 31, 1988, sec. F, p. 1-2.

Pinckney, Josephine. *Three O'clock Dinner.* New York: Viking, 1945.

South Caroliniana Library Collection.

Septima Poinsette Clark

Clark, Septima Poinsette, with LeGette Blythe. *Echo in My Soul.* New York: E. P. Dutton and Company. 1962.

Livingston, Mike. "Activist, Educator." *The State,* June 17, 1987.

Nejri, Itabarti. "Septima Clark." *The State,* June 11, 1987.

South Caroliniana Library Collection.

Modjeska Montieth Simkins

Ante Bellum: A New South Carolina Journal for Women. Summer/Fall, vol. 3, 1977.

Moniz, Dave. "I've Always Been an Independent Thinker." *The State,* March 9, 1986, pp. 48-51.

South Caroliniana Library Collection.

Woods, Dr. Barbara. "Advocate of the People: Modjeska Simkins." Marietta, Ga.: Southern Technial Institute, Nov. 6, 1985.

Personal interview. June 22, 1988.

Lucile Ellerbe Godbold

Weston, Elise. "Olympic Woman." *The State Magazine,* June 10, 1984.

News clippings.

Personal correspondence.

Personal memories of Miss Ludy as teacher, Columbia College.

Annie Green Nelson

McFadden, Dr. Grace Jordan. "Oral Recollections of South Carolina Afro-American Women." Richland County Public Library, March 14, 1988.

Nelson, Annie Green. *Don't Walk on My Dreams.* Spartanburg, S.C.: Reprint Company, 1976.

South Caroliniana Library Collection.

Personal interview. March 1, 1988.

Gwen Judson Bristow

Contemporary Authors. Michigan: Gale Research Co., 1976.

Bristow, Gwen. *Celia Garth.* New York: Thomas Crowell, 1959.

Bristow, Gwen. *Gwen Bristow.* New York: Thomas Crowell.

Augusta Baker

Personal interview. Jan. 31, 1989.

Biographical Directory of Librarians. 5th ed. Chicago: ALA, 1970.

News clippings. *Beaufort Gazette,* Feb. 8, 1988.

Sandlapper Magazine, April 1988.

Something About the Author. Vol. 3. Michigan: Gale Research Co., 1972.

"The Friendly Forum." Richland County Public Library, February 1988.

Juanita Redmond Hipps

Blassingame, Wyatt. *Combat Nurses of World War II.* New York: Random House, 1967, pp. 22–23, 31–32, 34.

Redmond, Juanita. *I Served on Bataan.* New York: Lippincott, 1943.

News clippings. *The State.*

Althea Gibson

Candee, Marjorie Dent, ed. *Current Biography.* New York: H. W. Wilson, 1957.

Frayne, Trent. *Famous Women Tennis Players.* New York: Dodd, Mead and Company, 1979, pp. 119–36.

Gibson, Althea. *I Always Wanted to Be Somebody.* New York: Harper and Row, 1958.

Ploski, Harry A., and Roscoe Brown. *The Negro Almanac.* 1st ed. New York: Bellwether Publishing, pp. 736–37.

Robertson, Max., ed. *The Encyclopedia of Tennis.* New York: Viking, 1974.

Hilla Sheriff

Dubose, Louise Jones. *South Carolina Lives.* Kentucky: Historical Record Association, 1963.

Bruce, Allison. "Dr. Sheriff: Health Pioneer." *The Spartanburg Herald-Journal,* June 22, 1986, sec. B.

South Caroliniana Library Collection.

Whitten, Kathleen. "The More I Did the More I Saw the Need." *The State Magazine,* Feb. 16, 1986, pp. 6–11.

Nancy Jane Day

Dubose, Louise Jones. *South Carolina Lives.* Kentucky: Historical Record Association, 1963.

Who's Who in Library Service.

Personal interview. January 24, 1989.

Elizabeth Boatwright Coker

Contemporary Authors. Michigan: Gale Research, vols. 45–48.

Lawton, Isobel Smith. "Elizabeth Boatwright Coker." *Sandlapper Magazine,* June 1970.

Milling, Chapman J. "Elizabeth Boatwright Coker and *Daughter of Strangers.*" *South Carolina Magazine,* November 1950.

South Caroliniana Library Collection.

Telephone interview. February 1989.

Index